1,000,000 Books

are available to read at

Forgotten Books

www.ForgottenBooks.com

Read online
Download PDF
Purchase in print

ISBN 978-1-333-23142-2
PIBN 10503367

This book is a reproduction of an important historical work. Forgotten Books uses state-of-the-art technology to digitally reconstruct the work, preserving the original format whilst repairing imperfections present in the aged copy. In rare cases, an imperfection in the original, such as a blemish or missing page, may be replicated in our edition. We do, however, repair the vast majority of imperfections successfully; any imperfections that remain are intentionally left to preserve the state of such historical works.

Forgotten Books is a registered trademark of FB &c Ltd.
Copyright © 2018 FB &c Ltd.
FB &c Ltd, Dalton House, 60 Windsor Avenue, London, SW19 2RR.
Company number 08720141. Registered in England and Wales.

For support please visit www.forgottenbooks.com

1 MONTH OF FREE READING

at

www.ForgottenBooks.com

By purchasing this book you are eligible for one month membership to ForgottenBooks.com, giving you unlimited access to our entire collection of over 1,000,000 titles via our web site and mobile apps.

To claim your free month visit: www.forgottenbooks.com/free503367

* Offer is valid for 45 days from date of purchase. Terms and conditions apply.

English
Français
Deutsche
Italiano
Español
Português

www.forgottenbooks.com

Mythology Photography **Fiction**
Fishing Christianity **Art** Cooking
Essays Buddhism Freemasonry
Medicine **Biology** Music **Ancient Egypt** Evolution Carpentry Physics
Dance Geology **Mathematics** Fitness
Shakespeare **Folklore** Yoga Marketing
Confidence Immortality Biographies
Poetry **Psychology** Witchcraft
Electronics Chemistry History **Law**
Accounting **Philosophy** Anthropology
Alchemy Drama Quantum Mechanics
Atheism Sexual Health **Ancient History**
Entrepreneurship Languages Sport
Paleontology Needlework Islam
Metaphysics Investment Archaeology
Parenting Statistics Criminology
Motivational

A SHORT MEMOIR OF THE PENNYMAN HOME AND FAMILY.

Arms. Gules a chev. erm. between three half spears with broken staves, or, headed argent.

Crest. Out of a mural coronet gu. a lion's head erased, or, pierced through the neck with a broken spear, as in the grant to James Pennyman, of Ormesby, 1 May, 1599, by William Segar, Norroy King-of-Arms. (See app. I. p.69).

Motto. Fortiter et Fideliter.

The Pennymans have been settled in the North Riding of Yorkshire for more than four hundred years. The will of John Pennyman, of Helmsley, was proved in 1498. Robert Pennyman, of Stokesley, in 1533 left to the church there "an Antiphonar in prynt." In 1588-9, William Pennyman, of Stokesley, left directions that he should be buried in the church of Ormesby, and left £10 to the poor of Stokesley and Ormesby. From that time onwards they have lived at Ormesby, and been described as Pennymans of Ormesby, as at the present day. It has not been by any means their only home; they have at times been owners of vast estates, scattered over the North Riding and elsewhere, and possessed places at Marske, Normanby and Beverley, all of which have long since passed out of their hands, and at Thornton, about four miles from Ormesby, where all trace of the house has disappeared, though the land is still theirs. But Ormesby has been for all these generations, and still is, their home; so perhaps it will be well to give a short description of the place and its surroundings, before going further into the history of the family. Probably many of the American Pennimans have never seen an English country house, and will therefore be the more glad to hear a little about the place which they believe to have been the home of their forefathers.

B

At the beginning of the last century the neighbourhood was solely agricultural. The estate reached to the river Tees, a few miles from its mouth, and one of the farm-tenants had to pay, in the days when rents were paid partly in kind, "two salmon fishes" to his landlord. Four miles from Ormesby there was, according to Graves' "History of Cleveland," published in 1808, " a township or chapelry of Middlesbrough, which consists only of four farm houses." Now the iron trade has come. Middlesbrough is its capital, and has a population fast getting on for 100,000; many of the villages in the district have become towns; the river is murky with smoke and resounds to the clang of machinery for miles of its course. Yet the little village of Ormesby has hardly changed. It still nestles among its trees, a pretty, peaceful spot for the busy worker from grimy Middlesbrough to cycle through on a summer's evening. Indeed if it were not for these cyclists and other traffic passing through the village, one might well fancy oneself in the depths of rural England. Within an afternoon's walk are the Cleveland hills, rising to heights of as much as 1,400 feet. From some of their summits there are views of unusual diversity, stretching over other hills, over the sea, which is but eight miles from Ormesby, over the course of the Tees fringed with chimneys and furnaces, and over miles of level plain to the west.

Ormesby Hall is a curiously built house. The older part, date unknown, is a square two-storied building, with a court-yard in the middle. This now contains the servants' offices, and one can easily see that they were built for the living rooms of the family; thus the kitchen measures 28 ft. by 20 ft. by 20 ft. The newer part, built by Dorothy, daughter and co-heiress of William Wake, Archbishop of Canterbury, (it is said to have been begun by her husband, who died in 1743, and to have been finished after her death in 1754,) is like the older, built of yellow sandstone, and is a solid square three-storied block, ugly from the outside, but most comfortable to live in, with many of the rooms panelled and with mouldings and decorations of a style that it is now difficult to obtain. This part contains the living rooms and bedrooms for the family and their guests. The whole house contains between fifty and sixty rooms. The two parts of it are placed corner to corner; many years ago there was no in-door communication between them; the food was all cooked in one part, and brought out of doors through the open-air to the other. This must have been delightful on snowy evenings. Now there are passages through, on both first and second floors.

The stables, built of the same sandstone, are extensive, having accommodation for over twenty horses. If the accommodation had been less, probably the family fortunes would have been greater; much good

ORMESBY HALL. SOUTH FRONT; OLDER PART OF THE HOUSE TO THE RIGHT.

Gc
92
P3
18

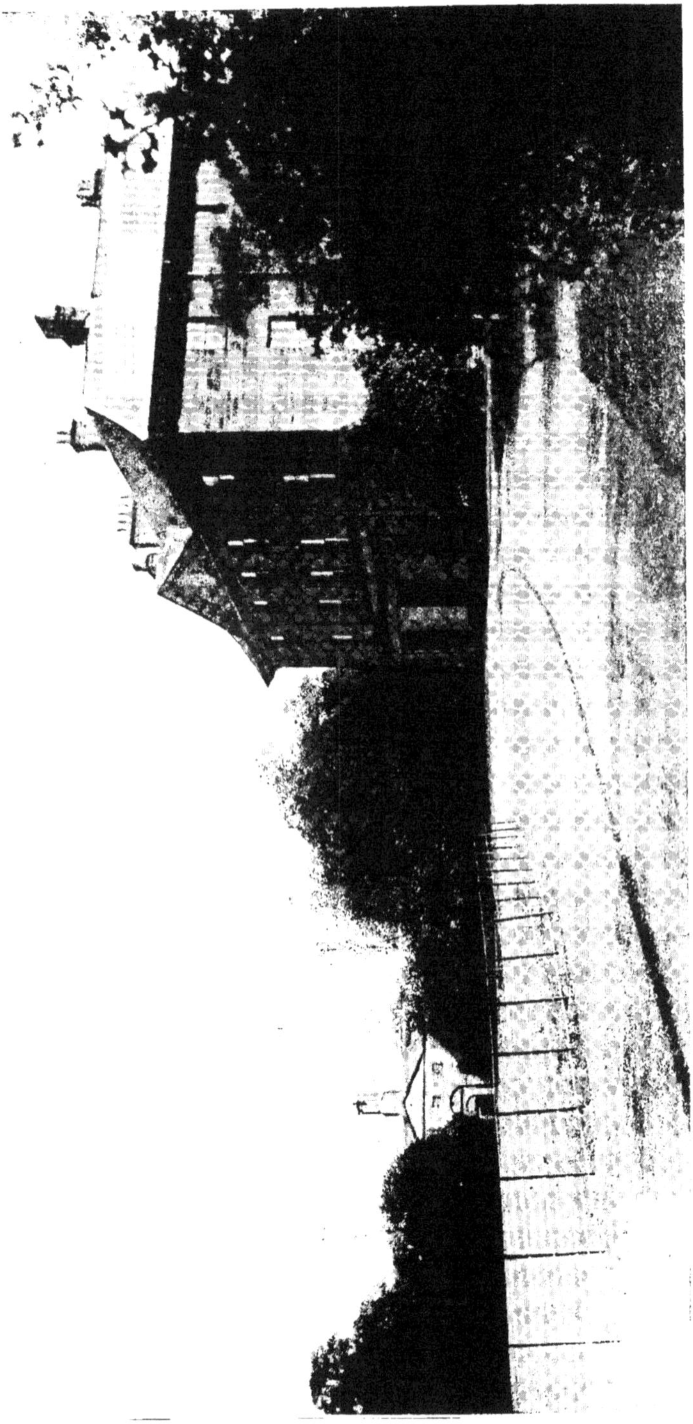

Pennyman money went in horse-flesh and other extravagances. Sir James Pennyman, who died in 1808, who is known as "The wicked Sir James," was a reckless spendthrift; even after his death, which took place at Richmond, Surrey, it cost over £500 to bring him home and bury him. His son, Sir William Henry Pennyman, the last of the baronets, found the estate in a ruinous condition. Yet even he thought it necessary to his dignity to go once or twice a year to Beverley in a coach and four.

The stable clock is more than a hundred years old. It is a fair time-keeper, and its bell, which is in a handsome cupola above the clock face, gives the time to the whole parish.

The Church, which dates from the Conquest, was partially re-built in 1810, and wholly re-built in 1875. It is stated in Domesday Book, compiled by William the Conqueror about 1080, that there were then in Ormesby a church and a priest. It is close to the Hall. The churchyard is particularly beautiful, surrounded entirely by fine trees standing in Mr. Pennyman's grounds.

These grounds are a delightful feature of the place. The paths through the woods must be nearly two miles in length, and whether one wants shelter from sun, rain, or wind, or it may be a quiet stroll apart from the hurly-burly of the busy district, or merely the pleasure of admiring the fine old beech, sycamore, and other trees that were standing there long before the first blast furnace was dreamt of, it is ever a fresh pleasure to walk along them. The garden too has delightful lawns and flower-beds, and the shrubs have been so well planted that it is full of pleasant places to sit in on a summer's day. The park is 100 acres in extent, and surrounded by a belt of wood. It gives a feeling of expanse, and prevents the place from looking shut in. There is a village cricket ground in it, and in winter, when the grass is short, a small golf green.

To turn from places to persons, the pedigree begins with Thomas Pennyman, of Stokesley, about seven miles from Ormesby. Then follows his son—

Ralph Pennyman, both without dates. Then his son—

Robert Pennyman, also of Stokesley, described in the Norroy King-of-Arms' Grant of 1599, as "esquire." Will dated 1533. He had three sons; of the youngest, Robert, we read in Drake's "History and Antiquities of York" (1736), in an account of the Rebellion of 1569 against Queen Elizabeth—"A. 1570. On Good Friday, March 27. Robert Pennyman, of Stoxley, gentleman, (and three others,) were drawn from the castle of York to the place of execution, called Knavesmire, and there hanged, headed, and quartered. Their four heads were set up on the four principal gates of the City, with four of their quarters. The other quarters were set up in diverse places in the country." The second son, James, is said, according to one story, to be the ancester of the American Pennimans (see app. N. p. 119). The eldest son was—

William Pennyman, variously described as of Stokesley, of Morton (a small township in the parish of Ormesby), and of Ormesby. He had two sons; the younger William Pennyman, of Stokesley, who by his will, dated 1588-9, directed that his body should be buried in the church of Ormesby; and the elder—

James Pennyman, of Ormesby, to whom William Segar, Norroy King-of-Arms, by grant dated 1st May, 1599, granted the crest still used by the family, in addition "to the shield or family coat of arms and insignia worn and used by the ancestors of his family from old time." (See app. I. p.69). He had two sons and a daughter of interest to our story. To take them in reverse order, his daughter Eliza or Elizabeth married, about 1612, Strangwayes Bradshaw, of Upsal, a township in the parish of Ormesby, the grandson and heir of Sir Richard Strangwayes, of Ormesby. Owing to this marriage Sir James Pennyman eventually became possessed of the Strangwayes estates in Ormesby. The latter family was one of considerable position; they held their Ormesby estates owing to the marriage of James Strangwayes with Ann, daughter and heiress of Sir Robert Conyers, of Ormesby, who was living in 14 Richard II., who held them by reason of the marriage of his grandfather Robert Conyers with Juliana, daughter and heiress of William Percy of Ormesby, one of the great Percy family, which owned land all over the North Riding; and they supplied High Sheriffs to Yorkshire no less than seven times between 1455 and 1539.

His son William Pennyman, Esq., of Marske, a small town on the sea coast, nine miles from Ormesby, may be of especial interest to some American Pennimans. He was one of the six clerks in Chancery, and married Ann, daughter of Robert Aske, of Aughton, co. York, and had, so far as the records in possession of Mr. Pennyman go, one son, Sir William Pennyman, Bart., who became a distinguished Royalist soldier, and Governor of Oxford. According to an American tradition he had another son, James Penniman, who emigrated to America, and became the founder of a family now consisting of over 2000 people in the States. But there is no proof of this story, and there is some ground for thinking that William Pennyman, of Marske, had only one son. (See app. N. p.119). He married Anne Atherton, who by descent was heiress of John, Lord Fauconberge, Earl of Kent, and through her became owner of the Manor of Marske. He built Marske Hall, a beautiful old house. He died without issue, and the house, which he only possessed in right of his wife, passed away from the family, and now belongs to Lord Zetland. He was High Sheriff of Yorkshire; and, according to Playfair's Baronetage, 1811, "was created a baronet in 1628. He was highly esteemed by Charles I.. who appointed him governor of Oxford, and colonel of a regiment of foot. Sir William was inferior to none in those convulsed periods in point of loyalty; and nobly maintained at his own expense two troops of horse and a company of foot." It is not surprising to hear that he died considerably in debt. He died in 1643, and was buried in Christ Church Cathedral, Oxford. The inscription on his monument there is given in app. L. p.10 . Lord Clarendon in his well known history (1707 Edition, Vol. II., pt. 2, Book VIII., p. 526) says of him:—" Upon the death of Sir William Penniman who had been governour of Oxford, to the great satisfaction of all men, being a very brave and generous person, and who performed all manner of civilities to all sorts cf people, as having had a good education, and well understanding the manners of the Court."

And now to go back to Sir William's grandfather, James Pennyman, of Ormesby, who has already been mentioned as obtaining a grant of a crest in 1599. His wife Ann appears to have been buried at Ormesby, May 28th, 1605, and he himself Nov. 20th, 1624, and his administration is given in app. C. p. 28. He was succeeded by his son, James Pennyman, of Ormesby, who married Catherine Kindersley or Kingsley. (See note on p.58 of app. F.) He was also a zealous loyalist, and suffered for it. The proceedings by which fines were levied on him and his son for their "delinquency" by the parliamentary government are given in app. J. p. 73. And White's " History of the North Riding," 1840, p. 687, says, " In the time of Charles I., James Pennyman, Esq., was a distinguished Royalist, and had so large a fine levied on him by parliament, that he was obliged to sell part of his estates for £3500; but it was re-purchased in 1770, by Sir James Pennyman, at the cost of £47,500, so great had been the improvement and advance in the value of landed property during the preceding century." He died in 1655, and his second wife, Mrs. Joan Pennyman in 1657. His will is given in app. C. p. 27. His second son was Thomas Pennyman, D.D., Rector of Stokesley, 1653-88, which place, however, he had to leave for a time during the war. The bridge over the Leven there, which is said in the North Riding records to have been called " Pennyman Bridge," may very likely have been named after him. His eldest son, James, afterwards

Sir James Pennyman, of Ormesby, was baptized there, March 6th, 1608. This "James Pennyman, Esq.," says Playfair, "was no less distinguished for his exertions in the cause of King Charles I., than the gallant Sir William Pennyman above mentioned; being a colonel in his army, and receiving the honour of knighthood for his bravery in the field. Both Sir James and his father were great sufferers for their faithful attachment, the sequestrators sentencing the latter to pay a fine of £700, besides compelling him to settle £100 per annum on the teachers of those times; and the former to a fine of £530. (See app. J. p. 73). These sufferings were not forgotten by King Charles II. after his restoration; and Sir James was created a baronet Feb. 22nd, 1663-4." His wife, Elizabeth, daughter and co-heiress of Stephen Norcliffe, was buried at Ormesby in April, 1678, and he himself a year later. His son—

Sir Thomas Pennyman, the second baronet, married Frances, daughter of Sir John Lowther, of Lowther (grandfather to Viscount Lonsdale). He was Lord Privy Seal to King William III. He was High Sheriff of Yorkshire 1702-3. He attended Quarter Sessions no less than 63 times; no slight feat in the days when there were no railways, and Thirsk, 30 miles off, was the place where they were most frequently held. His father attended 42 times, and his cousin William Pennyman 49 times. (See app. K. p. 95). He died in 1708. His son—

Sir James Pennyman, third baronet, was born in 1662, and succeeded in 1708. He is described as of Ormesby and Thornton, and lived mostly at the latter place, which is a hamlet in the parish of Stainton, about 4 miles from Ormesby. All trace of the house there has disappeared; but there is a small sketch of it in the British Museum in a collection of sketches of Yorkshire houses, made by Mr. Warburton. ("Journal of John Warburton," Lansdowne MSS., No. 911, 1718-19). He married in Nov. 1692, Mary, daughter of Michael Warton, Esq., of Beverley (by Susanna his wife, daughter of John, Lord Powlett of Hinton St. George, co. Somerset, and granddaughter of Michael Warton the elder, by his wife Catherine, daughter and co-heiress of Christopher Maltby, of Maltby, a hamlet in the parish of Stainton. This family had lived at Maltby for about 16 generations, from about 1112 to about 1612, or perhaps each date should be a few years later. Mr. Pennyman still holds some of the Maltby land in Maltby, though curiously it does not seem to have come through his ancestress, Catherine Warton. According to Graves' " History of Cleveland," p. 481, the Maltby lands had been divided some five generations previously, when one moiety passed by marriage to the Morleys of Normanby, and it is this moiety that Mr. Pennyman holds. To go back to Mary Warton, who married Sir James Pennyman, she became co-heiress to her brother Sir Michael

Warton, Kt. She died in 1727, and was buried at Stainton. From that time onwards till the death of the last of the baronets, the family had much to do with Beverley. They had a house there, and many of them were born there, or married or buried in the beautiful Minster there—often called a miniature of York Minster—and there are in it many Pennyman monuments. (See app. B. and L.) He died 17th Dec., 1745, aged 82, and was buried at Stainton.

He had issue his eldest son, James, who married Dorothy, daughter and co-heiress of William Wake, Archbishop of Canterbury, and died without issue in 1743, two years before his father. His widow died in London in 1754. By her will she directed a monument to be erected to her husband, apparently preferring that it should be done at her heir's expense rather than at her own. She built the newer part of the present house, as has been mentioned. (See app. O. p. 130.) It seems probable that she did so with Wake money, though after her death the house must go to the Pennyman and not to the Wake family. He had also—

Sir William Pennyman, fourth baronet, who died unmarried in 1768, and—

Sir Warton Pennyman Warton, fifth baronet, who married Charlotte, daughter of Sir Charles Hotham, of Scorborough, and had two sons, who both predeceased him without leaving issue, and nine daughters. He died in 1770. He had also Thomas Pennyman who died in 1759, and—

Ralph Pennyman, of Beverley, who died without succeeding to the baronetcy. He married Bridget, daughter of Thomas Gee, of Bishop Burton. He had issue, besides Dorothy Pennyman, who married the Rev. James Worsley, and will be mentioned presently, and two other daughters who both died childless,

Sir James Pennyman, sixth baronet. He was born at Eston in 1737, and married Elizabeth, daughter of Sir Henry Grey, Bart., of Howick. He was a most extravagant man, and ran through every penny that was not entailed, and had the pleasure of seeing his house in the possession of bailiffs. His picture was painted (as Mr. Pennyman) by Sir Joshua Reynolds, who charged 20 guineas for it, in 1760 or 1762, as appears from a letter from the late Tom Taylor, who was cataloguing Sir Joshua's pictures, to the late Capt. J. W. Pennyman. The portrait is now at Ormesby. He died at Richmond, Surrey, in 1808, and was buried at Stainton, at a cost of over £500. (See app. O. p.127). He had six sons and four daughters, every one of whom died without issue. His eldest son—

Sir William Henry Pennyman was the seventh and last baronet. He was born at Eston in 1764. He married Charlotte, daughter of Bethell

Robinson, of Catwick. He died 9th May, 1852, aged 89, and was buried at Beverley. He left the estate to his sister, Mrs. Robinson, for life. She only survived him for a few months, and died in the same year, 1852. On her death it passed under his will to his heir-at-law, James White Worsley.

As has been mentioned, Ralph Pennyman, of Beverley, the son of the third and father of the sixth baronet, had a daughter Dorothy. She married on the 17th Dec., 1761, at St. Cuthbert's, York, the Rev. James Worsley, rector of Stonegrave, near Hovingham, the son of Thomas Worsley of Hovingham, by Mary Frankland his wife, the great granddaughter of Oliver Cromwell. This family, a very old one, received in 1838 a baronetcy, which is still in existence. Their eldest son, Col. James Worsley, born 1764, died 1807, married Lydia, sister of Sir Thomas Woollaston White, Bart., of Walling Wells. Their eldest son—

James White Pennyman, on succeeding to the Ormesby estate, assumed, in compliance with the will of Sir William Henry Pennyman, by royal licence, dated 18th April, 1853, the name and arms of Pennyman. He married, 24th March, 1828, Frances, 3rd daughter and co-heiress of the Rev. James Stovin, D.D., rector of Rossington. She died 6th June, 1869, and he died 1st Feb., 1870. He had issue one daughter, Frances Maria, who married in 1855, Lt.-Col. Forbes Macbean, who commanded the 92nd Gordon Highlanders, and whose son, Forbes Macbean, has also commanded the same regiment; and one son—

James Stovin Pennyman, born 15th Oct., 1830. He married Mary Mackenzie, daughter of William Joseph Coltman and Philadelphia his wife, the sister of Sir William Worsley, Bart. They had issue, 2. Alfred Worsley Pennyman, a Lt.-Col. in the army, late of the 25th King's Own Scottish Borderers; 3. Frank Worsley Pennyman, who died in 1881, aged 17; 4. The Rev. William Geoffrey Pennyman, vicar of Bishopthorpe, who married Beatrix Jane Frances, daughter of Sir James Walker, of Sand Hutton, Bart., deceased, and has issue a daughter; Edith Mary, who married George Fraser Phillips, Major in the 14th Prince of Wales' Own West Yorkshire Regiment; and their eldest son—

James Worsley Pennyman, the present owner of Ormesby. He was born August 10th, 1856, and married 6th Oct., 1882, Dora Maria, 3rd daughter of Henry Frederic Beaumont, Esq., of Whitley Beaumont, in the West Riding of Yorkshire, for which Riding the latter was on several occasions Member of Parliament. He was a scholar of Trinity College, Cambridge, and took classical honours, and is a Justice of the Peace and Deputy-Lieutenant for the North Riding. He has two sons,

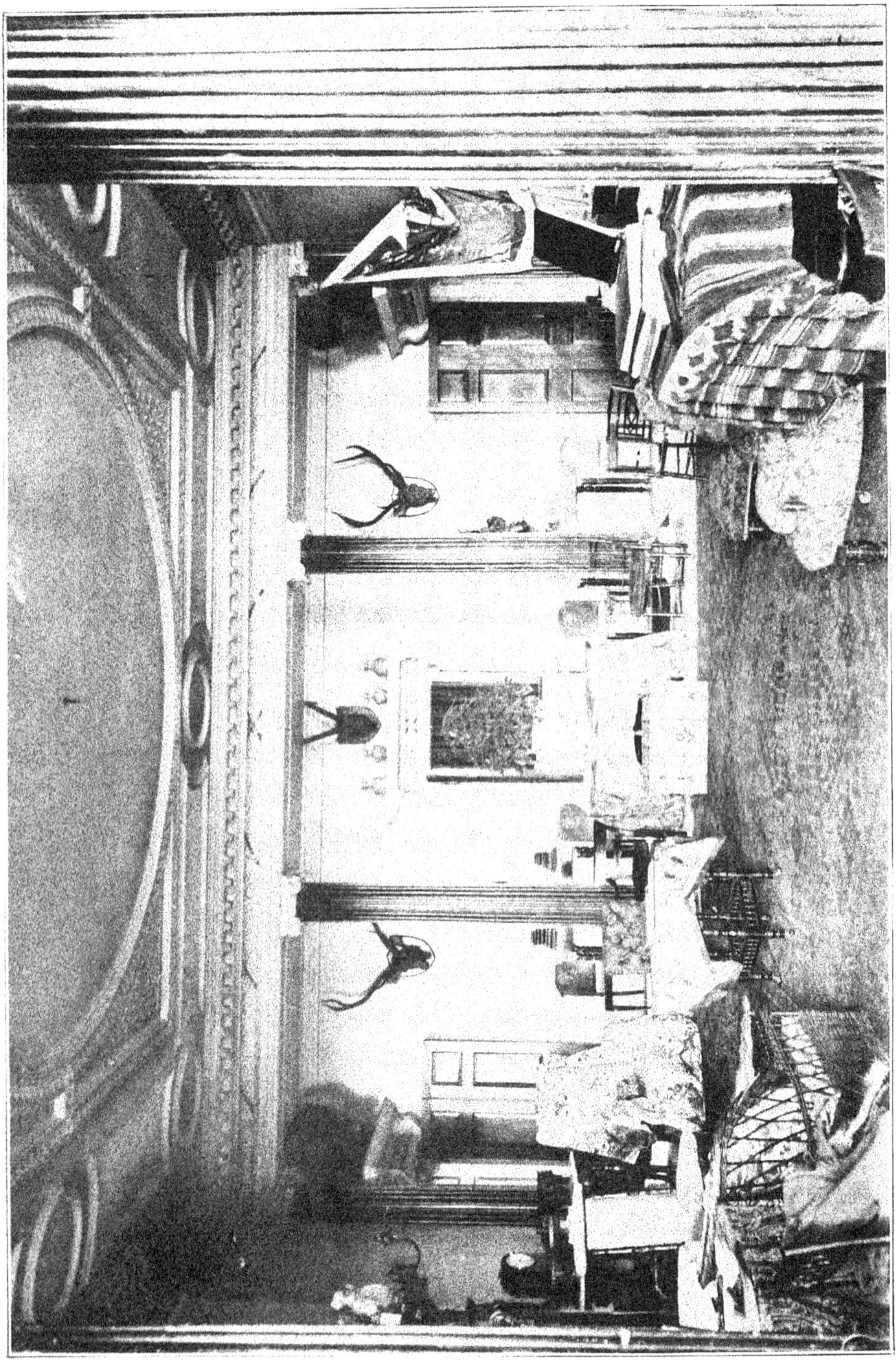

James Beaumont Worsley Pennyman, born 17th Dec., 1883, now an undergraduate at Trinity College, Cambridge, and Thomas Henry Pennyman, born 16th May, 1892, and one daughter, Mary Dorothy.

There are not many articles of interest at Ormesby. Sir William Henry Pennyman, when leaving the estate to his sister for life, left all his personal property to her absolutely, and she left all she had to her husband's relations, so that Capt. Worsley, as he then was, succeeded to bare walls, and, owing to the extravagance of the last Sir James, to farms in a ruinous condition, and a heavily mortgaged estate. He even had to bring an action at law to recover the title deeds of the estate. The oldest document in Mr. Pennyman's possession is the draft made in the Herald's Office for the grant of a crest to Mr. Pennyman in 1599; a translation of this is given in app. I. p. 69. The next oldest is an old parchment document in the shape of a roll, 9 in. wide, and 19 ft. long, written in latin in a very crabbed hand. It is a copy of part of the Pipe Roll, kept at the Record Office, and is a discharge to Sir William Pennyman, of Marske, who was High Sheriff in 1635. One of his chief functions was to collect certain moneys for the King, and on presenting his accounts and getting them passed for his year of office (Michaelmas 11 Chas. I., to Michaelmas 12 Chas. I.), he received this document as his discharge, which, as always when there were no arrears, ended with the words *quietus est*. Hence the phrase, "getting one's quietus."

Another document at Ormesby is a copy of a private Act of Parliament, passed in 1775, to confirm the partition of the estate of Sir Michael Warton, deceased, under his will dated 6th April, 1724. The Act recites that the three gentlemen making the partition were the representatives of the co-heiresses of Michael Warton, the last owner who left issue, that they employed valuers to divide the whole estates (which were very scattered and worth over £240,000, a large sum for those days) into three equal parts, not as yet appropriated to the three owners, "so as each share might lie together," that the particulars of the three estates were sealed up, marked 1, 2, and 3, and delivered to the custody of Robert Burton, of Lincoln's Inn; that the three owners met at Newark on 15th Dec., 1774, to draw lots, and agreed to proceed as follows:—
"That duplicates should be prepared by the said Robert Burton of the said three several numbers, which should be put into a glass or hat, and that the same should be respectively drawn or taken out thereof by some indifferent person......... And it was also further agreed that in order to prevent all disputes respecting the priority of the person to be entitled to receive the first, second, and third, of the numbers so to be drawn, the said proprietors should cast lots for the same ...... and ...... did appoint

Sarah Palethorpe, of Newark, aforesaid, spinster, of the age of 13 years, or thereabouts, to draw........." And the Act goes on to relate the actual drawing of the lot and to confirm the division so made. None of these lands now belong to Mr. Pennyman.

An old peg tankard, made for William Pennyman between 1578 and 1597, but not now belonging to the family, is described in app. O. p. 128.

This is all Mr. Pennyman has to tell about the family in England. Unfortunately, it is not rich in records. No doubt the pedigree gives many more names, younger sons and their wives, daughters and their husbands. To Americans these will be mere names; a Yorkshireman will find among them and others that have been mentioned, many names still well known in Yorkshire and the North Country, such as Norcliffe, Lowther, Hotham, Boynton, Bethell, Grey, and Beaumont. And now in point of numbers it has shrunk to very small dimensions. Neither Mr. Pennyman, nor his father, nor his grandfather, have ever come across anybody of the same surname. So there seems to be strong ground for supposing that there are only ten persons of the name in England.

APPENDIX A.

PENNYMAN ARMORIAL BEARINGS.

1. PENNYMAN: Arms. Gules, a chevron ermine between three half spears with broken staves, or, headed argent.
   Crest. Out of a mural crown, gules, a lion's head erased, or, pierced through the neck with a broken spear. (Granted to James Pennyman of Ormesby, 1 May 1599, by William Segar, Norroy). Motto, Fortiter et Fideliter.
2. NORCLIFF: Azure, five mascles voided in cross, or, a chief ermine.
3. WARTON: Or, on a chevron azure a martlet between two pheons of the field.
4. HANSBY: Azure, three shovellers close argent, a chief ermine.
5. MALTBY: Argent, on a bend gules three garbs or.
6. WORSLEY: Argent, a chief gules.
7. KIGHLEY: Argent, on a fess sable a fleur-de-lis or.
8. ARTHINGTON: Or, a fesse between three escaloppes gules.
9. EMPSON: Azure, a chevron between three crosses formies argent.
10. STOVIN: Barry of six or and gules, in chief a label of five points argent.
11. COLTMAN: Azure, a cross patonce, pierced of the field, or, inter four mullets pierced argent.

BEAUMONT ARMORIAL BEARINGS.

1. BEAUMONT: Arms, Gules, a lion rampant within an orle of nine crescents argent.
   Crest, A bull's head erased, quarterly argent and gules, the horns per fess, the dexter or and the second, the sinister or and the first.
   Motto: Fide sed cui vide.
2. LASCELLES (of Lascelles Hall, Kirkheaton, Huddersfield, West Riding).
3. HORTON (of Barkisland: Aggbrigg and Morley Wapentake, W.R.)
4. TURTON

As shewn in pedigree at Whitley Beaumont, compiled by William Radcliffe in 1828.

Gc
92
P3
18

APPENDIX B.

ENTRIES IN PARISH REGISTERS.

ORMESBY (commences in 1599).

1603. Sept. 19. James Pennyman and Catherine Kindersley* married.
1605. May 28. Anne wife of James Pennyman buried.
1606-7. Jan. 25. Anne dau. of James Pennyman junr. baptized.
1607. April 8. Anne dau. of James Pennyman buried.
✝ 1608. March 6. James son of James Pennyman baptized.
1609. June 17. Elizabeth dau. of James Pennyman junr. baptized.
1609. Aug. 20. Elizth dau. of James Pennyman buried.
1614. April 10. Thomas son of James Pennyman baptized.
1614. Aug. 10. James Pennyman son of Mr William Pennyman buried.
1615. April 19. Mary dau. of James Pennyman junr. baptized.
1616. June. 17. Mary dau. of James Pennyman buried.
1624. Sept. 2. William (?) son of James Pennyman baptized.
1624. Nov. 20. James Pennyman senr. buried.
1625. Dec. 19. Anne dau. of James Pennyman baptized.
1626. Nov. 2. Anne dau. of Mr James Pennyman buried.
1627. June 19. Audria dau. of Mr James Pennyman bapt.
1627. Nov. 9. Audria dau. of Mr James Pennyman buried.
1628. Aug. 24. William, son of Mr James Pennyman baptized.
1629. Nov. 26. Godfrey, son of James Pennyman baptized.
1631. Sept. 8. Joan dau. of James Pennyman nata et sepulta.
1631. Feb. 12. Godfrey Pennyman buried.
1632. Oct. 17. Joan dau. of James Pennyman baptized.
1632-3. May 3. William son of Mr James Pennyman junr. baptized [buried March 9].
1634. Feb. 28. Bradshaw, son of Mr James Pennyman baptized.
1640. Sept. 3. John Gibson Esqr. & Mrs Joan Pennyman married.
1651. Sept. 4. Joan dau. of Mr William Pennyman baptized.
1652. Aug. 15. James son of William Pennyman baptized.
1653-4. Feb. 23. Frances dau. of Mr William Pennyman baptized.
1655. Sept. 11. Elizabeth dau. of Mr. William Pennyman of Rounton baptized.

*See Note as to this name, at the end of Appendix F.

1655. Oct. 19. Mr James Pennyman of Ormsbie buried.
1657. April 11. Joane Pennyman the quondam wife of Mr James Pennyman buried.
1659. Aug. 18. Mrs Joane Pennyman wife of Mr William Pennyman buried.
1659. Sept. 24. Mr William Pennyman buried (19 August?).
1670. April 25. Robert son of Thomas Pennyman buried.
1672. Mch. 31. Mary Pennyman buried.
1678. April 8. The Lady Elisabeth wife of Sir James Pennyman buried.
1679. April 24. Sir James Pennyman Knt. and Bart. buried.
1694. May 1. Mr John Morland and Mrs Elisabeth Pennyman married.
1708. Aug. 3. Sir Thomas Pennyman Bart. buried.
1743. Dec. 23. James Pennyman Esq. buried.

Vide Inscriptions, Appendix L. 1.

SAINT MARY, SOUTH BAILEY, DURHAM.

1637. Apr. 7. James son of James Penniman gen. baptized.
1638. Apr. 13. James son of James Penniman buried.
1642. Aug. 29. Thomas son of Sir James Penniman knt. baptized.

KIRKLEATHAM.

1652. June 29. Mrs. Sara wife of Mr Thomas Pennyman buried.

STAINTON (commences in 1551.)

1673. Sept. 30. Charles son of Thomas Pennyman Esqr. baptized.
1675. Dec. 28. Charles son of Thomas Pennyman Esqr. baptized.
1677. July 1. Edward son of Thomas Pennyman baptized.
1677.   Edward son of Thomas Pennyman buried.
1691. March 1. William son of William Pennyman Esqr. buried.
1694. Jan. 27. William son of William Pennyman Esqr. baptized.
1695. June 19. William (?) son of James Pennyman Esqr. baptized.
1700. July 1. Warton son of James Pennyman Esqr. baptized.
1714. April 14. Marcia dau. of James Pennyman Knt. and Bart. buried.
1745. Dec. 24. Sir James Pennyman Bart. buried.

GUISBRO' (commences in 1661.) Baptisms and marriages searched to 1720, and Burials to 1731.

1677. June 21. Mr James Pennyman & Mys Elinor Loy was married.
1679. May 27. Elizabeth dau. of Mr James Pennyman baptized.

1680. Feb. 15. James son of Mr James Pennyman baptized.
1684. May 21. Elizabeth dau. of Mr James Pennyman buried.
1685. May 12. Katherine dau. of Mr James Pennyman baptized.
1686. Dec. 9. Frances dau. of Mr. James Pennyman baptized.
1690. March 17. William and Easter son and dau. of Mr James Pennyman baptized.
1690. Dec. 7. Mys Elisabeth Pennyman buried.
1692. Nov. 3. Elisabeth dau. of Mr James Pennyman baptized.
1695. Sept. 29. Richard, son of James Pennyman, gent., baptized.
1696. March 9. Edward son of James Pennyman, gent., baptized.

ESTON.

1658. Dec. 16. Mr William Pennyman son of William and Joan Pennyman, baptized.
1693-4. Feb. ult. Edward son of Mr William Pennyman of Normanby, born 14 Feb. (buried 21 May 1694.)
1702. Jan. 20. Frances Pennyman dau. of William Pennyman Esqr. buried.
1712. Oct. 17. Rev. William Consett & Elisabeth Pennyman married.
1718. Dec. 12. William Pennyman Esqr. buried.
1719. March 22. Richard Pennyman son of William Pennyman Esqr. buried.
1722. March 17. Captain Consett & Mrs Johanna Pennyman married.
1737. Aug. 18. A. P. born betwixt 3 & 4 afternoon.
1737. Dec. 6. Sir James Pennyman, Bart., born.
1764. Jan. 14. William Henry Pennyman born.
1808. Apr. 15. Sir James Pennyman, Bart., died at Richmond in Surrey nr. London 27 March: buried at Stainton 15 April.

PONTON PARVA, co. Lincoln.

1747. James son of James Pennyman Esq. and Dorothy his wife, born Aug. 30, christened Sept. 28.
1748. Mr James son of James Pennyman Esqr. and Dorothy his wife, ob. Dec. 10, buried Dec. 12.
1750. (A.) Elizabeth wife of Henry Pennyman Esqr. of Grantham, ob. March 22, buried March 27, aged 66.
1754. (B.) Henry Pennyman Esqr. of Grantham ob. Aug. 20, buried at Ponton Aug. 29.
1754. William son of James Pennyman Esqr. and Dorothy his wife, born Aug. 11, christened Sept. 16.

1756. John Henry son of James Pennyman Esqr. and Dorothy his wife, born Feb. 3, christened March 19.
1764. James Pennyman Esqr. ob. Nov. 3, buried Nov. 6.
1795. John Henry Pennyman Esqr., aged 40, buried 25-6 Nov.; ob. at Bath, Nov. 15; Major of the Cinque Port Light Dragoons [M.I.] In another register book it is thus stated . . . . son of James and Dorothy Pennyman, born Nov. 26, 1795, aged 39 years, died at Bath, Nov. 13th.
1806. William Pennyman son of James Pennyman and Dorothy his wife, aged 52 years, bur. July 22, died at Brighton, July 12. [M.I.]
1810. Mrs Dorothy Pennyman died Jan. 8, was buried Jan. 13, aged 85 years.
    A. Elizabeth wife of Henry Pennyman, sister of William Daye Esqr. [M.L]
    B. Henry Pennyman Esqr. son of Sir Thomas Pennyman Bart., of Ormesby in Cleveland, Yorkshire, who died Aug. 21, 1754, aged 74.

Vide Inscriptions, Appendix L. 4.

BEVERLEY MINSTER.

1759. August. Thomas Pennyman buried.
1766. March. James Warton Pennyman baptized.
1767. July. Ralph Pennyman baptized.
1769. May. Henry Grey Pennyman baptized.
1770. Jan. Sir Warton Pennyman buried.
1770. Oct. Charles Pennyman baptized.
1773. Jan. Hannah Pennyman baptized.
1776. Jan. Charlotte Pennyman baptized.
1777. March. Mary Pennyman buried.

Vide Inscriptions, Appendix L. 2.

ALL SAINTS', NORTH STREET, YORK.

1698-9. Feb. Mr James Pennyman, gent., buried.
1745. Aug. 13. Mrs Pennyman, widow, buried.
1748. Sept. 5. Mr William Pennyman, buried.
1758. March 27. Mrs Easter Pennyman, buried.

STOKESLEY (commences 1571.)

1584. Aug. Robert Burton and Ann Pennyman married the 18 day.
1660. June. Thomas Pennyman was restored to the Rectory of Stokesley.

1661. May. Ann dau. of Doctor Pennyman babtised ye 27th day.
1661. Jan. Ann dau. of Doctor Thos. Pennyman buried ye 9th day.
1662. Oct. Sarah dau. of Doctor Pennyman baptised ye 5th day.
1663. Oct. Marmaduke & Mary children of Dr. Tho. Pennyman then ye Parson of Stokesley baptisd ye 20th day.
1664. Feb. Marmaduke son of Dr. Thomas Pennyman buried ye 11th day.
1665. Mar. John ye sonne of Doctor Thomas Pennyman baptised ye 8th day.
1666. Oct. Thomas ye Son of Thomas Pennyman Esqr. of Easby, baptised ye 11th.
1667. May. Mary dau. of Dr. Tho. Pennyman of Stokesley buried ye 27th.
1667. July. Edward son of Dr. Pennyman of Stokesley baptised ye 27th.
1667. Oct. Edward son of Dr. Tho. Pennyman buryed ye 1st day.
1667. Nov. Wm. ye son of Tho. Pennyman of Easby Esqr. baptised ye 28th.
1668. Nov. Richard son of Doctor Pennyman baptised ye 19th.
1668. Dec. Elizabeth dau. of Thos. Pennyman of Easby Esq. baptised ye 17th.
1669. Feb. Robert son of Thos. Pennyman of Easby Esqr. baptisd ye 8th.
1669. Mar. Thomas son of Dr. Thos. Pennyman now Rector of Stokesly buryed ye 22nd.
1670. Feb. Mary ye doughter of Thomas Pennyman Esqr. baptised ye 21 day.
1672. July. Katherin ye doughter of Pennyman of Easby bapt. ye 8 day.
1678. Aprill. Thomas ye son of Mr. James Pennyman of Stokesly baptised ye 2d. day.
1688. Sept. Thomas Pennyman D.D., and Rector of Stokesley buried the 25th day.

(And many later entries.)

HOVINGHAM (commences in 1642: the registers for 1649, and 1668-72, and the baptisms for 1740 omitted.)

1654. June 23. Charles son of Thomas Worsley, baptized.
1658. Feb. 15. Thomas Worsley senr. of Hovingham buried.
1664. Nov. 5. Thomas Worsley of Hovingham buried.
1677. April 19. Thomas the son of Ebenezer Worsley baptized.
1678. Sept. 13. Robert son of Ebenezer Worsley baptized.

APPENDIX B.

1680. July 1. Mary dau, of Ebenezer Worsley baptized.
1680. Sept. 11. John Worsley of Hovingham gent. buried.
1681. Nov. 30. Elizth. dau. of Ebenezer Worsley baptized.
1683. March 5. Mr. Robert Worsley buried.
1684. April 1. Ebenezer son of Ebenezer Worsley baptized.
1684. June 12. Mary dau. of Thomas Worsley baptized.
1686. Nov. 28. Thomas son of Thomas Worsley baptized.
1688. April 5. Henry son of Thomas Worsley baptized.
1688. Nov. 29. Ebenezer son of Ebenezer Worsley buried.
1689. April 15. Arthington son of Mr. Thomas Worsley baptized.
1690. June 3. Robert son of Thomas Worsley esqr. baptized.
1690. Aug. 7. Henry son of Thos. Worsley Esq., buried.
1691. Aug. 10. Robert son of Thos. Worsley Esqr., buried.
1692. May 26. Arthington son of Thos. Worsley Esqr., buried.
1693. Feby. 3. John Worsley buried.
1698. March 22. Thomas son of Ebenezer Worsley buried.
1701. Sept. 29. ffrances ffoljambe esqr. and Mrs. Mary Worsley married.
1706. July 9. Thomas Woodward and Elizabeth Worsley married.
1711. Dec. 20. Mrs. Mary Worsley the wife of Thos. Worsley Esqr. senior, buried.
1712. Dec. 4. Mrs. Mary Worsley dau. of Thos. Worsley Esqr. junior, baptized.
1713. May 14. Susanna the wife of Mr. Ebenezer Worsley buried.
1715. Jan. 4. Mr. Ebenezer Worsley buried.
1715. May 18. Thomas Worsley, esq., buried.
1715. Sep. 21. Elizabeth, daughter of Thomas Worsley, Esq., baptized.
1722. Aug. 28. James son of Thos. Worsley Esqr. baptized.
1722. Sept. 4. Mary wife of Thos. Worsley Esqr. buried.
1735. May 31. Marmaduke Constable of Wassand Esqr. and Mrs. Mary Worsley dau. to Thomas Worsley Esqr. of Hovingham, married.
1735. Aug. 2. Charles son of Thos. Worsley Esqr. buried.
1736. July 4. William son of Thos. Worsley Esqr. buried.
1737. July 13. Thos. Robinson Esqr. and Mrs. ffrances Worsley dau. of Thos. Worsley Esqr. married.
1750. March 2. Thos. Worsley Esq. buried.
1769. Sept. 28. Septimus son of Thos. Worsley Esqr. baptized.
1770. June 4. Frederick son of Thos. Worsley Esqr. buried.
1778. Dec. 22. Thos. Worsley Esqr. buried.

LOUTH, co. LINCOLN. (Baptisms lost from 16 Sept. 1692, to Sept. 1693.)

1689. Feby. 28. Mary dau. of Mr. Samuel Worsley and Mary his wife, baptized.
1690. Dec. 28. Samuel son of Mr. Samuel Worsley and Mary his wife, baptized.
1690. Dec. 31. Samuel son of Mr. Samuel Worsley buried.
1691. May 28. Mr. John Worsley and Mrs. Elizabeth Cracroft married.
1693. Oct. 7. Thomas son of Mr. Samuel Worsley and Mary his wife, baptized.
1694. Aug. 17. Samuell son of Mr. Samuel Worsley and Mary his wife, baptized.
1694. Sept. 8. Samuell son of Mr. Samuell Worsley, buried.
1698. May 2. William son of Mr. Samuel Worsley and Mary his wife baptized (born April 16).
1698. May 11. William son of Mr. Samuel Worsley buried.
1700. Nov. 10. Elizabeth dau. of Samuell Worsley, apothecary, buried.
1701. July 8. Samuel son of Mr. Samuel Worsley, apothecary, and Mary his wife, baptized (born July 6).
1727. April 11. Mr. John Barker and Rosamund Worsley married.

ROSSINGTON.

1799. March 24. Rose dau. of Rev. James Stovin, rector of this place, and Eleanor Charlotte his wife, baptized (born Feby. 23).

Gc
92
P3
18

Gc
92
P3
18

APPENDIX C.

PENNYMAN WILLS & ADMINISTRATIONS.

(All at York, except the three marked * which are in London.)

Date of Probate.		Reference to Abstract.
1498.	Penyman, John, of Helmsley ...	No. 1.
1533.	Pennyman, Robert, of Stokesley	,, 2.
1595.	Pennyman, William, of Stokesley	,, 3.
1625.	Pennyman, James, of Ormesby, *Adm.*	,, 4.
†1628.	Pennyman, William, of Marske, esqr.	,, 5.
*1649.	Pennyman, Sir Wm., of Marske, knt., *Adm.*	,, 6.
*1655-6.	Pennyman, James, of Ormesby, esq.	,, 7.
*1660.	Pennyman, William, of Tampton, gent.	,, 8.
1698.	Pennyman, James, of Hutton Lockars	,, 9.
1708.	Pennyman, Sir Thomas, of Ormesby, bart. ...	,, 10.
1720.	Pennyman, William, of Normanby, esq.	,, 11.
1721-2.	Pennyman, Annabella, of Normanby, widow	,, 12.
1741.	Pennyman, William, of Normanby, esq., *Adm. de bonis non.*	,, 11.
1743.	Pennyman, James, of Normanby, esq., *Adm.*	,, 13.
1745.	Pennyman, Sir James, of Thornton, bart.	,, 14.
1755.	Pennyman, Dorothy, of Ormesby, widow	,, 15.
1758.	Pennyman, Esther, of York	,, 16.
1759.	Pennyman, Thomas, of Bp. Burton, but late of Beverley, esq., *Adm.*	,, 17.
1759.	Pennyman, Sir James, of Thornton, bart., *Adm. de bonis non.*	,, 14.
1768.	Pennyman, Sir William, of Thornton, bart.	,, 18.
1770.	Pennyman, Sir Warton, cf Beverley, bart. ...	,, 19.
1770.	Pennyman, Thomas, of Bp. Burton, but late of Beverley, esq., *Adm. de bonis non.*	,, 17.
1808.	Pennyman, Sir James, of Ormesby, bart.	,, 20.
1852.	Pennyman, Sir William Henry, of Ormesby, bart. ...	,, 21.

(*Note.—In the following Abstracts and Copies of Old English Wills, the original spelling is retained.*)

1. JOHN PENNYMAN, of Helmsley.
    Dec. 31, 1498. [Vol. iii. fo. 333]

    Daughter, Isabel Dowson, 5/-. Daughter, Joan Pennyman, 20/-. Cousin, Joan Pennyman, 3/4. Residue to wife Isabel, and William, Robert, and Richard Pennyman, executors.

    Proved at York, Jany. 25, 1498-9.

2. ROBERT PENNYMAN, of Stokesley.
    28 Dec. 1533. [xi. 69]

    To be buried in church of Stokesley. To the same churche "an Antiphonar in prynt." "Also I will have one preste for one yere." Wif Margret my landes in Bushe and in Stokesley for lif, to bring up my children, and after her death to my sonne and here Willm. Residew to wif Margret, and childn. Willm., James, Robert, Jane, and Margerie Pennyman, executors.

    Witnesses :—Sir James Bartrom, Richd. Pennyman.

    Proved at York 11 March 1533-4, by Margret Pennyman the relict, and William, James and Johan *(sic)* Pennyman, the childn. of decd., power being reserved for Robert and Margerie.

3. WILLIAM PENNYMAN, of Stokesley.
    21 March 1588-9. [xxvi. 204]

    To be bur. in church of Ormesby. Poore of Stokesley and Ormesby £10 at discretion of my brother James Pennyman. Maister James Strangeways, 4 old Angels. Sisters Mary, Margaret, and Averell £10 each. Sister Margery £6 : 13 : 4. Nephew Thos. Addison £10. Nephew Henry Addison my dunne geldinge and best cloake. Sister Isabel £20. Nephew Wm. Nelson £20. Sister Ann £3 : 6 : 8. Childn. of brother James (his son Robert excepted) £100 amongst them. Uncle Robert Manne 40/-. Brother White, an old Angell. Servant James Crane 20/- a yere for 13 yeres, and he then to have £10, or same annuity to continue. Cosen Henry Manne my dunne meare (mare). Ralph Sleighton my best dublet. Nicholas Conyers a pair of my hoose. To each of my brother James his servants, (Hindson excepted,) 5/-. Cosen Warde, an Angell. Cosen Marwood my bay nagge. Nephew Robt. Pennyman, son and heir of my brother James Pennyman, all my lands at 21, and also £150. Wm. Hindson and Miles May 30/-. Residue to brother James Pennyman, sole executor.

      Witnesses:—Wm. Marwood, Henry Addison.

            Proved at York, 12 Dec. 1595, by the executors.

4. JAMES [Jacobus] PENNIMAN, of Ormsbie.
    5 May 1625.   [Cleveland Act Book.]

Administration of the goods etc. of deceased was granted to James [Jacobus] Bradshaw, junior, of Upsalles co. York.

5. WILLIAM PENNYMAN, of Marske, co. York, esquire.
    24 Feb. 1625.

In the Name of the Father and of the sonne and of the holy ghost Amen I Willm Pennyman of Marske als Maske in Cleveland in the Countie of Yorke Esquier one of the six Clarks of the high Court of Chauncery being of good health and pfect memory thancks be therefore giuen to almightie god doe make this my last will & testamt in manner and forms following First I giue and bequeath my soul to almightie god beseeching him in the bowells of his Mercie and for the merritts of Jesus Christ my only Sauior and redeemer to pardon and forgiue me all my sinnes and to receiue my soule into his heavenly kingdome And my bodie to be buried where it shall please god to call me wthout any pompe or vaine ostentacon And for the setling of such worldly estate as it hath pleased god to bestowe vpon me First my desire and care is that my debts may be duely and wth all convenient expedicon satisfied and discharged And to this end and purpose I doe giue and deuise to my welbeloued brother Mr James Pennyman of Ormsbie Esquire and to my loueing cousin Mr James Morley Esquier and to their heires and assignes for ever all my messuages land tenemt and hereditamts in the towne and Borough of St Albanes in the Countie of Hertfs and in the parish of St Peters St Michaels and Sandridge nere the said Towne of St Albanes in the said Countie of Hertf and also all my messuages lands tenemts and hereditamts in Vpsalles in the pish of Ormsbie in the said Countie of Yorke and also all my messuages lands tenemts and hereditamets in Brotton and in Inglebie and Berwicke vpon Teese in the said Countie of Yorke and also all my leases for yeeres of any lands

tenemts tithes and hereditamts wch I haue hold and enioy wthin the
Realme of England   And also all my goods and chattells household
stuffe plate jewells and debts and also the three hundred pound wch
is to be paid by decree of the High Court of Chancery by my
Successor in the offices of six Clarks to my Executors   All these
things I doe devise vnto them vpon this trust and confidence (and
not vpon condicon) that they and the Survivor of them and the
heiress of the Survivor of them shall wth as much convenient speede
as they can sell all the same or so much thereof as neede is and wth
the money wch shall arise by sale thereof or otherwise by meanes
thereof pay all my owne iust and true debt wch will appeare vnto
them by a little paper booke wherein the same are sett downe wch
is in my deske in my study in the six Clarks offices   And after my
debts paid I will that the Residue of the money wch they shall
receiue and such of the things aforesaid as shall remaine vnsold they
shall giue deliuer and assure the same to my sonne Wm Pennyman
if he be then liueing and if he be dead Then to such issue of his
bodie as shalbe then liueing   And if there be no such issue liueing
then to my loueing wife Anne Pennyman if she be liueing   And if
she be deade then to my two godsonnes Wm Pennyman my brother
James his sonne and to Wm Bradshawe my sister Bradshawes sonne
to be equally deuided betweene them to helpe to make them porcons
And also I doe will and devise to my said loueing wife Anne Pennyman   All my lands tenemts and hereditamts in Ormsbie and Caldi-
cote in the said Countie of Yorke for terme of her life and after her
death the remainder thereof to my said sonne Wm Pennyman and
the heires of his bodie begotten and for default of such issue the
remainder thereof to my said loueing brother Mr. James Pennyman
and his heirs for ever   And whereas I am now seised of an estate
taile of the greatest pte of the Mannor of Marske als Maske and
Ridcar wch will come to my said sonne Wm by discent and make
vp a full third parte and more of all my lands and tenemts I now
stand seised of wch doth enable me to devise all the residue of my
other lands and whereas I haue bought sundry other parcells of land
of seuerall psons in Maske Ridcar and Cotome wch are not yet
entayled I doe therefore now will deuise and bequeath all my said
other lands tenemts and hereditamts whereof I now stand seised in
Fee simple in Marske Ridcar and Cotome to my said sonne William
Pennyman and to the heires of his bodie begotten   And for default
of such issue to my said loueing brother Mr James Pennyman and
his heires for ever   And of this my said last will and testamt I doe

make and ordaine my said loueing brother James Pennyman and my said loueing Cosen James Morley my Executors and doe giue to each of them fiue pounds to buy each of them a peece of plate In Witness whereof I haue herevnto sett my hand and seale the xxiiiith day of February 1625 And in the first yeere of the raigne of or soveraigne Lord Charles by the grace of god King of England Scotland Fraunce and Ireland Defendor of the faith &c Wm Pennyman Sealed deliuered and published in the prsence of Willm Nelson Tho. Manwood Willm Addison Wm Comondell

> Proved 14th May 1628 in the Prerogative Court of Canterbury, 14th May 1628, and in the Prerogative Court of York, 2 Oct. 1628.

6. SIR WILLIAM PENNYMAN, of Marske, knight.
1649. [P.C.C. Act Book, fo. 106.]

Administration of the goods &c. of deceased was granted to Edmund Savage.

7. JAMES PENNYMAN, late of Ormsby, co. York, Esq.
29 June 1655.

To be buried in the chancel of Ormsby Church, as near my father as may be.

Son James Pennyman, my bay stone colt, called Fenwicke; my lease in Ormsby which I hold of Mr. Jervase Elwes; all my tables and stools in the hall at Ormsby; all my tables and cupboard in the parlour with three chairs and six stools of Turkey work, which were in the said room before my late marriage, my brewing vessels, my cistern in my kiln, etc.

And whereas I have lately sold my house at Richmond for £35, to be paid to me 11 Nov. next, if I die in the meantime, my son James shall receive the same.

Son Thomas, £20 per annum, out of the £40 per annum I have out of the lands of my cousin Bradshawe in Upsalls; and if my cousin Bradshawe pay my executors £500 (as he has the choice of doing), then my son Thomas shall receive £200 thereof.

Son William Pennyman and his heirs my land I bought in his name from Sir John Gibson, called Samley Hill; my leases of tithes in Marton and Normanby, he paying thereout yearly to my sister Sartan £10; my lease from my brother Kingsley in Upsalls; £40 per annum during the term out of the grant of £80 per annum made to me by my son-in-law Gibson* for 20 years, and after my death my son Gibson to be discharged of the other £40 per annum. " Also I give *him* the residue of my rent I have in Upsalls of my cousin Bradshawe, £20 by year; and if my cousin redeem that rent, then he (my son Thomas being paid £200) is to have the remaining £300.

Son John Pennyman, £100, provided I pay not so much for him to my son Thomas, which I promised him, being the use of £500 lent by my son Thomas to my son John for three years.

Daughter Gibson my wrought bed, my brooch, and my old black saddle nag.

To Allan Sartan, whom I brought up, 100 marks, and he to be kept by my executors till he have some livelihood.

To the poor of Maske, Normanby, and Marton, £10 each place, and £10 yearly for ever to the poor of Ormsbye out of the parcel of land I lately purchased of Robert Tompson in Stoxley.

To my friends Mr. George Grainge of Eston, and Nicholas Pearson of Ormsbye, £5 each; to my servants that sit in the hall at meat 10s. each; and to my servants that sit in the kitchen at meat 5s. each.

Residue of my goods, rent charges, etc., taken from my cousin, Mr. John Garnett of Arlesbye, Mr. Leonard Beckwith of Handale Abbey, Mr. Foster of Durham, etc., I bequeath to my loving wife Joan and my son William, executors.

Witness:—J. Gibson, Robert Jackson his mark, Allan Sarten, John Sidgwicke.

> Proved in the Prerogative Court of Canterbury [Register Berkley, 10], 2 January, 1655-6, by Joan and William Pennyman, the relict and son of deceased, the executors named in the will.

8. WILLIAM PENNYMAN, late of Tampton, co. York, gentleman.
    20 September 1659.

To be buried in Ormesby Church, as near my father as may be.

All my estate, real and personal, to my brothers, John Gibson of Welburne, co. York, Esqr., and John Pennyman, of London, woollen draper, whom I make my executors, upon trust as I shall direct.

Daughter Joan £1000 at eighteen, and her mother's best necklace of pearls, the little enamel ring, and my mother's wedding ring.

---

*See Appendix O, No. 1, for an interesting letter to this John Gibson, who married Joane Pennyman, daughter of the testator.

Daughter Frances £1000 at eighteen, my other pearl necklace, which was her mother's, the cupid jewel, and my mourning ring.

Daughter Elizabeth £1000 at eighteen, the star jewel, yellow stone ring, and link ring.

Son William £1200 at twenty-one, and the diamond ring which Mrs. Metcalfe gave me.

To Sir James Pennyman and his lady, £1 apiece; to my sister Gibson £3; to my brother, Mr. Thomas Pennyman, and his wife £1 each; to my brother, John Pennyman's wife £1; to each of my nephews and neices 10s.; to my brother-in-law, Mr. Lewis Stockett £5; to Mrs. Mary Metcalfe £4; to Mrs. Jane Brames £5; to Mr. Alan Smallwood £5, and to his wife £1; to Mr. Remington £1; to my cousin Alan Sartan, of Yarum, £1; to my cousin, Mr. Richard Yoward, £1; to my cousin Margaret Tod £1; to my maid Elizabeth £1; to each of my servants 5s.; to Margerie Cotham £3 yearly for life.

I give my executors power to dispose of my wearing apparel as they think fit, and of any other of my goods up to the value of £10.

My plate is to be reserved for my children (save what I give to my son James), and my linen is to be equally divided among them. All my books (save such books and manuscripts which relate to surgery and physic, which I give to my daughter Joan,) and also the diamond ring my mother gave me, my wife's wedding ring, the pewter with my arms on it, my flower wrought silver cane, and my silver knob spoons, I give to my son James.

I will that my executors give my son James the residue of my estate at his age of twenty-one, and if he die before that age, then my son William shall have his portion, and the £1200 I gave to my son William shall be equally distributed among my surviving children.

Executors 40s. apiece.

Witnesses :—Lewis Stockett, Mary Metcalfe, Jane Brames, Elizabeth Turner, William Sartan, Allan Sartan.

> Proved in the Prerogative Court of Canterbury [Register Nabbs, 252], 11 September 1660, by John Gibson, of Welburne, Esqr., and John Pennyman, citizen of London, the executors named in the will.

9. JAMES PENNYMAN, of Hutton Lockars (Lowcross), co. York.
21 Nov. 1698, 10 Wm. III. [lxii. 240]

Wife £10 and a "great flowred silver tankard marked wth. the Pennyman's arms and the set of silver castors marked wth. the

Pennyman's and Saunder's armes " for life or widdowhood, and then to my son Thomas a silver tankerd marked T.P.S., and silver spoons marked T.P.E. Son James a silver tankerd marked wih. the Pennyman and Dorrell armes and silver spoones marked T.E.P. Son John a silver tankerd marked J.E.P. Dau. Catherine silver cup and spoon marked T.E.P. & spoon marked J.E.P. Dau. ffrances silver Cawdell cup marked T.S.P., two salts marked J.E.P. and silver spoons marked R.T. Dau. Easter a silver porringer and cup marked H.P., silver tumbler marked J.E.P., gilded spoone marked J.H.E.S., and another spoon marked H.H. Son Richard various silver plate—described—marked respectively T.E.P., T.S.P., P.T., and E.P. Son John, one Jacobus of gold. Son William, one double guinea. Wife, a clock. Poore labourers of Hutton Lockars and Gisbrough, 50/-. Poore of All Saints, North Street, York, 50/- Son Thomas my messes in Hutton Lockars wch. I hold for three lives of the Lord Archbishop of Yorke, he paying out of that my estate to my childn. by the first venter, James, John, Catherine and ffrances £120 apeece at 21 or marre, and to my younger childn. by the second venter, Richard, Edward, and Esther £220 between them. Son Willm. £500 pursuant to the articles of marriage wth. my now wife.

Sr. Thos. Pennyman, knight and barronett, and Sr. Wm. Hustler, knight, to be supervisors.

Residue to son Thomas, executor.

Witnesses :—Richard Pennyman : Rowland Sawer : Thos. Pennyman.

No Probate in Register. 1697-99.

10. Sr. Thomas Pennyman, of Ormesby, barronett.

6 Dec. 1700. [lxv. 5]

Recites settlement made on marriage of son James Pennyman, who married on 18 Oct. 1692, Mary one of the daurs. of Michael Waiton of Beverley, she being of the Parish of S. Giles in the Fields, co. Middlesex. Younger sons Thomas, Charles, and Henry. Allaine Catchpoole of the City of London, who hath married my daur. Catherine, £500.

Witnesses :—Mary Morley : James Dunning : James Sayer.

Proved at York Sept. 14, 1708.

11. WM. PENNYMAN, of Normanby, esquire.
    30 July 1717.   [lxxiv. 474]

Wife Annabella. Daughters Annabella Pennyman, and Elizabeth wife of Wm. Consett. Joanna Pennyman. Grandson Wm. Consett. Son Richd. Pennyman, executor.

> Proved at York 19 Feby. 1719. And on July 1741, administration of the goods etc. of deceased, not administered by Richd. Pennyman esqr., his son and administrator, was granted to Annabella his widow, Joanna wife of Matthew Consett esqr., and Elizabeth wife of Wm. Consett, clerk, his daughters, next of kin, and residuary legatees. [Rydall Act Book.]

12. ANNABELLA PENNYMAN, of Normanby, widow.
    29 April 1721.   [lxxvi. 114]

Daughters Johanna Pennyman, Annabella wife of Richd. Morley, and Elizabeth Consett.

Witnesses :—Margt. Chapman : Richd. Conyers.

> Proved at York 17 Jany. 1721-2.

13. JAMES PENNYMAN, of Ormesby, esquire.
    23 Feby. 1743.   [Cleveland Act Book.]

Administration of goods etc. of deceased was granted to Dorothy Pennyman, widow, his relict.

14. SIR JAMES PENNYMAN, of Thornton [parish of Stainton], co. York, Bart.
    24 April 1743.

Whereas by my marriage settlement portions were to be raised under a term of 500 hundred years for my younger children and I have already paid to my 4 younger sons Wm., Thos., Warton, and Ralph £1000 apiece for their portions, the said term to be void, and as to the lands by me purchased in Thornton, Stainton and Maltby, co. York, I charge same with payment of £5 yearly for ever to such poor persons within the constablery of Thornton as my eldest son James or the heir male of my family shall think fit objects of that charity. And as to the rent charge by me purchased and issuing of lands at Stainton and as to all my personal estate, I give same to Geo. Vane of Long Newton co. Durham, esqr., James Hustler of

Aclam co. York, esqr. and Ralph Robinson of Ormesby co. York, esqr. upon trust for each of my sons and the wives of my sons Jas., Warton and Ralph £20 for mourning.

Eldest son James to endeavour to procure lease to make a vault in Stainton church for my burial there in a leaden coffin handsomely finished, and for my funeral expenses I give him £600.

Trustees to erect in sd. church 3 marble monuments of a proper size for my late dear wife my daughter and myself cut and placed in such a manner as those over Sir Ralph Warton and Ralph Warton esqr. in St. Mary's Church in Beverley, and my great grandfather's monument to be repaired where it is defaced, and such tombstones to be erected over my grandfather and grandmother and my father and mother at Ormesby as that of my said great grandmother with proper inscriptions upon them.

My plantation at Thornton to be enclosed with a brick wall 3 yards in height with pillars 7 yards distant from each other jutting half a yard from the wall.

A schoolhouse to be erected in the Town Street of Thornton, and I charge my said lands in Thornton Stainton and Maltby with payment of £20 yearly for the maintenance of a schoolmaster to teach gratis the poor children of Maltby Thornton Stainton and Ormesby to read write and cast accounts, which said master and children shall always be nominated by the heir male of my family, with power to remove same for any misdemeanour.

All my lands &c. in Middleham, Coverham, Spennithorne, Great Aycliffe, Ingleby Arncliff, Whorlton and Ormsby, I give to my eldest son James for life, with remainder to his sons by Dorothy his now wife successively in tail male, with remainder to my 3rd *(sic)* son Thos. Pennyman in tail male, my son Warton, and my youngest son Ralph, succeeding in tail male, with remainder to my own right heirs for ever.

Said George Vane, James Hustler, and Ralph Robinson to be **exors.**

Witnesses :—Henry Robinson, John Robinson, and David Burton.

Codicil 1. 24 April 1743. I have paid off a mortgage of £2500 to Mr. Silvester Pettit and have taken an assignment in the names of Sir Wm. Hustler and my sons Warton and Ralph Pennyman in trust for myself. I give same to my executors in trust. I forgive my son Ralph £250 he owes me. Same Witnesses.

Codicil 2. 5 May 1743. My third son Thos. my lands in Middleham which I bought of Mr. Digby, lands called the Garths bought of Mr. Kilvington, and Ten Mile Hill bought of Humber Smith, and my moiety a field in Middleham called the Dovecoat field which I hold in common with Thos. Scott. Same Witnesses.

> Proved at York 21 Jan. 1745. And on the 12 Nov. 1759, Administration of the goods, &c., of deceased, not administered by Thomas Pennyman, esqr., son and administrator, was granted to Warton Warton, esqr., son of the deceased.
>
> [Prerogative Act Books.]

15. DOROTHY PENNYMAN, of Ormsby, co. York, widow.

4 August, 1753. [xcix. 65.]

If I depart this life above 50 miles from Ormsby, to be interred according to such directions as I shall leave in writing, and for want of such directions at discretion of my brother-in-law, Thomas Strode, esq. But if I die at any place not more than 50 miles from Ormesby, then in Ormsby church in the vault there with my late dear husband, without any ffuneral pomp of escutcheons, &c., or any bearers or attendants save my own servants and Mr. David Burton, of Yarm. Vicar of Ormsby certain mourning and a piece of Portugall Gold, value 36/-, for his burial ffee. Each of my servants now in Livery proper, mourning, and to those in Livery and others not hereby otherwise provided for and rewarded, half-a-year's wages, beyond what shall be due to them, and in lieu of mourning for my Livery servants, 4 guineas each. A large Black Marble Stone to be laid over the vault in memory of my husband and myself, with low iron pallisades round it. *To my brother-in-law Thos. Strode, esq., the Rev. Mr. Goodricke (vicar of Aldbrough), and Mr. John Catlin, of London, gent., all my manors, lands, &c., and all my personal estate, upon trust to sell and place out £700 (£600 whereof is in the hands of Pemberton, of Sunderland) in trust my niece Dorothy Pennyman. Niece Dorothy Pennyman 12 guineas for mourning and her late Uncle's gold watch and such pictures and crayons as were drawn for him, and the plate, &c., set down in a paper of my own handwriting. Niece Love, of Bristoll, my own picture and frame now in my sister Strode's possession, and the picture of my late Most Rev. and Dear Father, now in my house at Ormsby. Servant Mary Gray £200 and £10 a year for life, and my apparel and house

---

* In a draft will dated 21st June, 1753, in Mr. Pennyman's possession, this clause and several other formal trust clauses are erased, and the will was proved as in this abstract.

linen. Servant James Swailes £100 and £5 a year for life, and my best riding horse. Servant Dorothy Swailes £10. Late servant Catherine, now wife of Joseph Hunter, of Ormsby, 4 guineas. Poor of Ormsby £100. £100 to certain Charities at discretion of executors. Inasmuch as proper decencys are wanted for the Communion Table in Ormsby Church, I give a good and strong table cloth with 2 napkins to the same, also my gilt cup and cover if approved by the Ordinary. Godson Love 7 guineas for a ring. Precise directions as to furniture and fittings, &c., of house. Niece Etheldred Lynch £40 as a marriage present for her tea table, also my black-japaned leaved skreen at Ormsby, being my own work, and certain old china in her mother's possession. Nephew John Lynch £20 on entering Holy Orders. Brother Strode 10 guineas for a ring. Rev. Mr. Goodricke £5 for a ring. John Catlin, of London, gent., and the said David Burton £25 each. Said Strode, Goodricke, and Catlin, to be Exors.

Witnesses:—Joshua Greezbie, Geo. Cook.

Codicil, 24 June, 1754.

Bequests of various pieces of furniture, &c. (described at length) to nieces Mary Lynch, Catherine Lynch, and Hester Elizabeth Lynch; nephew John Bennett; godson and great nephew Martin Seymour; niece Dorothy Pennyman, and brother Thomas Strode, esq.

Witnesses:—Elizabeth Hustler, Easther Horner.

April, 1754. A note of goods, &c., I give to my niece Dorothy Pennyman.

Proved at York, in the year 1755.

16. ESTHER PENNYMAN, of York, spinster.

24 March, 1758.   [cii. 82.]

To be buried in the grave of my mother in the par. church of All Saints, North Street, York. Friends, Mrs. Pawson, widow, and Mrs. Stainton, wife of Mr. Robert Stainton, saddler. Poor of S. Martin's, Micklegate, £3. Sarah Baildon, 10/-. Poor of All Saints, North Street, 40/-. Cousin Mr. Fras. Saunders, apothecary, £10. Goddaughter Mary Stainton, £10. Elizth. Whisker, daughter of Mr. Daniel Fras. Whisker, decd., £10. Mrs. Ann Varley, £2 2s. Residue to my brother Edwd. Pennyman, of Holborn, London, saddler, executor.

Witnesses:—Thos. Varley, Timothy Mortimer.

Proved at York, Aug. 1758.

17. THOMAS PENNYMAN, of Bishop Burton, and late of Beverley, esquire.

25 Aug., 1759.   [Prerogative Act Book.]

Administration with the will annexed of the goods, etc. of decd. was granted to Warton Warton, esqr., his brother; Mary, wife of Wm. Berry, gent., niece and sole executrix; Sir Wm. Pennyman, Bart., and Ralph Pennyman, esqr. (two of the surviving brothers, and Carlotta Warton, Margt. Warton, Harriott Warton, and Mary Pennyman, spinster, four of the nieces, and residuary legatees, having first renounced.

10 May, 1770.   [Prerogative Act Book.]

Administration of the goods not administered by Warton Warton, esq. (afterwards Sir Warton Pennyman Warton, Bart.), since deceased, was granted to Sir James Pennyman, bart., nephew and now next of kin of the said Thos. Pennyman, decd. Mary Warton (afterwards wife of Wm. Berry), niece and sole executrix, etc., etc. (as before), having first renounced.

18. Sir WILLIAM PENNYMAN, Bart., of Thornton-in-Cleveland.

24 Jan., 1763.

Nephew James Pennyman, esqr., all my lands, &c. in tail male, with remainder "to the right heirs of the ffamily of the Pennyman's for ever." All my mortgages, securities, and ready money to be laid out in purchases of land for the use of my said nephew in tail male, with remainder as above. My two brothers and sisters and all my nieces except Mary (   ) whose residence I am informed is at Bristol, £10 cash for mourning and mourning rings. Godson John Henry Pennyman £5 to be laid out in a ring. Kinswoman Attilanta Pennyman, daughter of Doctor Charles Pennyman, my late uncle, deceased, £10, if living at the time of decease, whose brother John Pennyman, if living, is in the West Indies. Mr. David Burton, of Yarm, £10 and a mourning ring. My housekeeper Mrs. Driver £8 above all wages, and £10 more if living with me at my decease, and the choice of my wearing apparel, and the remainder to John Tureman, the Butler. Poor of Ormsby £5, and Thornton Matton and Stainton £5. Funeral to be made in a private manner, and to be carried to the grave by six of my tennants, to whom I order hatbands and gloves, and all such tennants as shall appear at my ffuneral to have gloves, and that I may be buried in some convenient part of the Church with a decent Monument placed over me with this Inscription:—" Hic jacet Dominus Willielmus Pennyman, Baronetus, Qui obiit anno, ætatis suæ." This monument to be placed opposite to my ffather's in Stainton Church, and inclosed with Iron Rails. Residue to my nephew James Pennyman, esq., sole exor. Brother Ralph Pennyman, esq., Wm. Bethill, esq., and Henry Masters, esq., and Mr. David Burton, of Yarme, to be trustees. To the rest of my godsons 5 guineas each, to be laid out in a ring or any memorial of me.

Witnesses:—Tho. Ward, Peter Coats, Wm. Garbut.

Codicil 1. Mr. Burton £20 for receiving the interest of the Securities he procured for me.

Codicil 2. Mr. Robert Burton £10, and to be a Trustee in case of his ffather's death.

Codicil 3. £50 yearly to be paid out of my estates to keep the house, &c., which I dwell in, and the gardens, &c., in perpetual repair and in good order.

Proved in the Prerogative Court of Canterbury,
4 May, 1768, by the executor,
and also in the Prerogative Court of York.

19. Sir WARTON PENNYMAN WARTON, of Beverley, co. York, Bart.

1 Jany, 1790.   [cxiv.] 12.

Wife Charlotta Warton, executrix. Chas. Hotham, of South Dalton, esq., and Robt. Burton of the Inner Temple, trustees. Grandson ffrancis Boynton £1000 at 21. Granddaughter Martha Stapilton £1000 at 21 or marre. Wife Charlotta £200 a year for life. Daughter Mary Berry. My six daughters Charlotta, Mary, Margaret, Harriott, Caroline, and Diana. Elizth. Lister, now an apprentice wth. Mrs. Lalame, milliner, in Leicester ffields, London, £500.

Witnesses:—John Dickinson, Robt. Caruthers, Geo. Sonley.

Proved at York, 30 Jany, 1770.

20. Sir JAMES PENNYMAN, of Ormsby, baronet.

1 June, 1801.

Wife Dame Mary Pennyman all my real and personal estate, and I appoint her executrix. Witnesses:—Conrade Coulthurst, Fredk. Langloh, and Wm. Fairbanks. (Republished and declared by

Testator, 16 Oct., 1805. Witnesses:—Tho. Lloyd, James Simmons, and John Winter Cuthbert. Also again 14 Nov., 1806. Witnesses:— Tho. Lloyd, James Smart, and Samuel Cuthbert.

    Proved in the Prerogative Court of York, 2 July, 1808, by Dame Mary Pennyman, widow, the executrix.

21. Sir WILLIAM HENRY PENNYMAN, of Ormesby, and of Beverley, bart. 30 May, 1848.

All my lands, &c., at Beverley and in the East Riding to my niece-in-law, Charlotte Jackson, spinster, now residing with me. To Wm. Wharton Robinson, of Oxford, Solicitor, and George Shepherd, of Beverley, Solicitor, during the life of the said Charlotte Jackson, an annuity of £250, upon trust for her. Also the following annuities for life:—Joseph Knaggs, my groom, £5; Elizth., wife of Jacob Stothard, of Ormesby, farmer, £30; Hannah Sayer, of Ormesby, spinster, £5; Ann Hind, of Ormesby, widow, £5; Eleanor Bowser, of Guisbro,' widow, £6; Fanny Hutton, of Thornton, widow, £9; Thos. Close, of Ormesby, tailor, and Ann his wife, £6 10s., all charged on my lands, &c. (except at Beverley and East Riding). All my other manors, lands, &c., to said Trustees for a term of 2000 years upon trust, to pay my debts and legacies, and with remainder to my sister Frances Harriet Robinson, widow, for life, with remainder to her sons successively, with remainder to my own right heirs for ever, they taking the surname of Pennyman only and the arms of my family. My plate (described) including that of my late wife Charlotte Pennyman and of the late Bethell Robinson to my said sisters Charlotte and Frances Harriet. Bequests to Beverley Dispensary, and several other charitable institutions. My said two sisters, executrixes.

Witnesses:—J. Williams and John Myers.

    Proved in the Prerogative Court of York, 28 June, 1852, by the executrixes.

Gc
92
P3
18

Gc
92
P3
18

APPENDIX D.

PENNYMAN NOTICES IN OTHER WILLS.

1. Note by the late Rev. C. Norcliffe of "A Will bearing upon the pedigree of Pennyman of Ormesby, which should be preserved as evidence of the match with Cleseby."

1550. Oct. 28. Will of Leonard Cleysby of Cleysby. Mentions wife Ellin, son John, daughters Marjerie, Anne and Mary Cleysby, Brother Arthur Cleysby, supervisors, Rawffe Cleseby, William Cleseby clerke, George Jacson, Jamys Conyers, and brother William Pennyman.

Inventory taken on day of death.

2. [Archdeaconry Court of Richmond. Register C. fo. 37 (61).]

Will of ROBERT BURNET,* of Ayreholme upon Tease.

4 July 1557.

In the name of god amen. the fourth day of the month of Julye in the yere of our lorde god 1557 That I Robert burnet of the hill house in the pishe of Ayreholme uppon Teise in the countie of Yorke yowman being of hole mynde and in good and pfite Remebrance laude and praise be unto almightie god maike & ordeyne this my psent testament concernyng herein my last will in maner and forme folowing That is to say First I comende my soule unto Almightie god my maker and redemer to our ladye saint Mary and to all the companye in heaven And my bodye to be buried within the pishe churche of Eyreholme with my mortuarie & oblacons dew and accustomed First I bequethe to the hye altar theare xx^d. Itm towards the Repacons vj^s viij^d Itm for forgitting tithes iij^s iij^d Itm I will that all suche dettes & dewties as I owe of Right or of Conscience to any person or persons be well & trulie contented and paid by myne executors hereafter namyd or els be ordened for so to be paid without any deley or contrediction And after my detts paid and my funerall expens pformed I will that all my goods cattells &

---

*His daughter Agnes married James Pennyman. See the will of his widow Elizth. Burnet. [No. 6 in this Appendix.]

detts shalbe devided into thre equall partes, wherof I will that Elisabeth my wiff shall have one equall parte to hir owne vse of all my goods cattells & detts after the laudable costome of the contre belonging And the secunde parte equall of all my goods cattells & detts I give to my childering laufullie begotten That is to say John Burnet Willm Robert Jayne Elizabeth & Agnes my children Equallie to be devided emonge them And to be delyued vnto them when they shall accomplishe and come to their lawfull ages of xxj yeres or els be maried And if it fortune any of my said children to decease (which god defende) before they accomplishe their said ages and before that time be not maried, That then I bequethe his or her parte soo deceasing to the other of them surviuyng to be delyued vnto them when they shall accomplishe ther said Ages or els be maried And the thirde Equall parte of all my said goodes Cattells and detts I resue to myne executors therwith to pforme my legacs & bequestes here after naymed First I bequeth to Mr. Markingfeld my best yong horse desiering his maistershippe to be good maister vnto my wiff & childringe Itm I bequeath to my sonne Willm Burnet towards his exhibicon the closse called brotle closse. Itm I bequethe to my sone Robert the lease and tearme of yeares of the close called the west feilde lieng & being within the towne & Feildes of Ereholme and my signet Itm I bequethe to Jayne burnet Elisabeth burnet & Agnes burnet my childering xxx[h] towards their marieges Equallie to be devided emonge them Itm I bequethe to Jayne Burnet my Eldest doughter xiij[h] vj[s] viij[d] Itm I bequethe to Janet Brere a newe Riall, to Agnes Bucke a newe Riall, to Willm Wormley a nev riall, to s[r] John Fawcet x[s]. Itm I bequethe to John bucke a stotte, to Ellys husband a qwye, to Isabell Branson a whye, to Anne Wrightson a whye, to Margaret Syme a whye, to Miles Weddelt a whye, to Jane Wormley a Whye, to Dorothe Wormlie a whie, to Elisabeth buck a Whye, to Margaret Wormlie a yowe & a lame, to Robt. Frear a yowe & a lame, to Roger Runket a lame, to Willm Coot a lame, to James Fiear a lame, to Loore Symson a lame Itm I bequeth to John Eshe & Margaret his wiff x[h] to thentent and uppon condicon that they shall clerelie remytt and Release all their title & Interest that they ought to clame or have by reason of their executorshipp Itm I will that my said wiff shall have myne house wherin I nowe dwell during her widowhed And as soon as and when as she shall be assured or maried to any other man that then I will that the lease & terme of yeares I give to John burnet my Eldest son for the proffett & furtheraunce of the noneages of my childering The residewe of all my goods cattells & debts after my detts paide my funerall expenses pformed And theis my legacs & bequests contented in this my present testament fulfilled I wholie give to Elisabeth my wyff and childering whome I make myne executours And my mynde and intent is that Thomas Markingfeld esquyer Richarde Brere gentilman Willm Wormlie yoman whome I make supvisors of my will And I give to Mr. Markenfeld an old Riall to Richarde Brere and to Willm Wormlye to aither of them an angell of goulde for their laboure in that behalf desiering them to ouse and governe my childering during ther noneages I bequethe to John burnet my son one messuage in Stowkylaw yerelie Rente x^s And I utterlie revoke all & cuye other former testaments wills legacs bequests by me in any wise before this tyme made Thees Witnesse Richarde brere Thomas wrightson John barker John Beitheson Curet the day & yere above written.

Proved 21 July 1557 by Elizabeth Burnet, the executrix named, with power reserved, &c., &c.

3. 1577. Feb. 28. Will of JAMES CONYERS of Osmotherley. Gives to William Bowes' children Christopher and Faith, and to young William Bowes vj^s viij^d each, to be paid by Bartholomew Pennyman; Mary Pennyman 40s.; wife Johane Conyers.

4. 1580. Will of WILLIAM BOWES of Ellerbeck, leaves to Clement Pennyman 40s.

5. 1580. Will of JOHAN, widow of James Conyers of Osmotherley. Bartholomew Pennyman a witness.

6. 1586. Will of ELISABETH BURNETT of the Hill house in the parish of Eriholme upon Tease, 1 Nov., 1586. Son Jhon Burnett all my right, etc., in Hillhouse and th' one halfe of Eastfeilde. Son Robert Burnett my house in the East feilde. Son William Burnett xiij^{li} vj^s viij^d. Son Robert Burnett xx^{li}. 2 daurs Jane Andersonne and Agnes Peneman xx^{li} each. Anne Peneman, my sonne in law James Pennyman his daughter iij^{li} vj^s viij^d, and to every of his other children a stirke or xx^s. Elizabeth Burnett my son William his daur iij^{li} vj^s viij^d, and to every his other children a stirke or xx^s. Son William Burnett his wyfe, a Kowe and a calfe. Daughters and daur in lawe Jane Andersonne, Elinor Burnett, and Agnes Peneman, to everye of them an angell. Jhon Eshe one filly stage, and to Jane Eshe his sister iij^{li} vj^s viij^d, and to everye of the other childn of my

daur Margaret Metcalfe a yowe or vj^s in money. Robt. Wormeley and Wm. Lawsonne x^s. each. God-daur Anne Dodsworth a yowe and a lame or v^s.

Proved in the Archdeaconry Court of Richmond.
(Eastern Deaneries. Will not now to be found in the Registry.)

7. 1646. Will of RD. HARRISON, of Ormesby, dated 5 July, 1646, and proved at York, 26 Aug., 1646 (unregistered), gives *(inter alia)* to my mistress Mrs. Joane Pennyman, Mr. William Pennyman, Mr. John Pennyman, Mrs. Joane Pennyman their sister, Mr. Thos. Pennyman my master his son, and Mr. Thos. Pennyman son of Sir James Pennyman, 50/- each; my fellow servants 12d. each; residue to my loving master Mr. James Pennyman, exor.

8. 1743. Will of WM. GEE, of Bp. Burton, esq. 1743. Dated at the camp of Aschaffenburgh (York Wills, lxxx—lx, 300). Mentions brother Ralph Pennyman and sister Bridget Pennyman.

9. 1746. Will of THOS. GEE, of Bp. Burton, esq. 1746. (York Wills xciv. 315). Gives remainder in lands to grandson James Pennyman, son of Ralph Pennyman, and my daur. Bridget Pennyman, if he shall change his name to Gee.

Gc
92
P3
18

APPENDIX E.

NOTES OF SOME PENNYMAN ABSTRACTS OF TITLE.

No. 1, 2, and 3 are in Mr Pennyman's possession ; No. 4 is in the Hailstone Collection of MSS. in the York Minster Library.

1. ABSTRACT OF TITLE of Sir James Pennyman, bart., only son of Ralph Pennyman, esqr., and only heir male now living of Sir James Pennyman, late of Thornton, bart., his grandfather decd., to a farm in East Upsall in Cleveland.

   1685. Thomasin Wilson of Stokesly, widow, and Constable Bradshaw of Nunthorpe, esqr., to Sir Wm. Hustler of Acklam, kt., and another.
   Down to 1735, no Pennyman's, mostly Mewburnes.
   1736. John Mewburn to Sir James Pennyman of Thornton, bart.
   1738. Ditto to ditto
   1743. Probate of will of Sir James Pennyman bart., the grandfather.

2. ABSTRACT OF TITLE to estate at Tampton or Tanton.

   1712. Esther Pennyman of York, wid. of James Pennyman of Hutton Lockars, gent., decd., and Wm. Pennyman of Bishopthorpe, gent., their son and heir, to Mary Savile of York, widow.
   1729—1732. Same parties.
   1743. Probate of will of Sir James Pennyman.
   1745. Thos. Pennyman and Wm. Pennyman.
   1752. Edwd. Keating of London, weaver, and Ann ux., only surviving child and heir of Wm. Pennyman decd., 1st pt., Edwd. Pennyman of St. Andrew's, Holborn, sadler, 2nd pt., Thos. Pennyman of Sir James Pennyman, 3rd pt., and Sir Wm. Pennyman bait., Warton Warton esqr., and Ralph Pennyman esqr., the three other surviving sons of sd. Sir James Pennyman, 4th pt., and Thos. of Durham esqr., 5th pt.
   1770. No Pennymans.

3. SCHEDULE OF DEEDS belonging to Lady Pennyman. (Mr. Pennyman has not these deeds.)

Sadberge. 1678. Thos. Garmansway to Thos. Pennyman.

1706. Thos. Croft to James Pennyman esqr.

...... Chas. II. Admission of Sir Thos. Pennyman, bart., to copyholds.

13 Queen Anne. Admission of Sir James Pennyman.

1747. Admission of Sir Wm. Pennyman.

Stainton. Robt. Willcock to Sir Thos. Pennyman.

Hutton juxta Rudby. 36 Charles 2. Robt. Armstrong to Sir Thos. Pennyman.

Stokesly. 33 Chas. 2. Wm. Gibbon to ditto.

14 Chas. 2. Settlement on marre of Thos. Pennyman with Frances Lowther.

Cold Kirby. 1744. Admission of Sir James Pennyman on surrender of Robt. Raikes, Fulthorp.

1755. Probate of will of Dorothy Pennyman.

Lands in *Tunstall, Sadbergh,* and *Stanfray.*

1651. Sir James Pennyman and Thos. Pennyman.

1667. Sir James Pennyman.

1675.   Ditto

1618. Thos. Wilson and James Pennyman.

1631. *Martyn,* co. York, James Pennyman.

1672. Wm. Pennyman and Thos. Pennyman.

1681. *Ormsby.* Sir Thos. Pennyman.

1683. Sir Thos. Pennyman. " Demise of Ferry Hill, co. Durham."

44 Eliz. *Ormsby.* Roen Bradshaw to James Pennyman. Release of all claims to lands at Ormsby.

1671—76. *Hutton Rudby.* Robt. Armstrong to Sir James Pennyman.

Sadberge. 1670--75. Sir James Pennyman.

Ormsby. 1603. James Pennyman, 1st pt., Wm. Kyndersley, 2nd pt., and James Pennyman, the son, and another, 3rd pt. Settlement on marre of James Pennyman with Kath. Kyndersley. Lands in *Ormsby.*

1604—6. James Pennyman.

1618.   Ditto   junr.

1631. Wm. Pennyman. Lands in *Ingleby Barwick.*

1632. James Pennyman.

1665—76. Thos. Pennyman. *Stokesley.*

1679. Sir James Pennyman. *Sadberge.*

1681. Oct. 11. Wm. Gibbon and another to Sir Thomas Pennyman. Conveyance. *Stokesly.*

1681. James Pennyman. *Stokesly*.

11 Car. 1. James Pennyman and Thos. Harrison and others. Feoffment of Manor of *Ormsby*.

1662. James Pennyman.

1662. Lord Easby to Sir James Pennyman. Lease of *Easby* for 7 yrs.

1665. Sir James Pennyman of Stokesly.

Stokesly. 1662. Sir James Pennyman.

1665—72. Thos. Pennyman.

1675. Sir James Pennyman of Thornton.

1609. *Ormsby*. Thos. Stockton to Sir James Pennyman. Feoffment.

1672. *Thornton*. Thos. Pennyman.

1679. Sir Thos. Pennyman.

1741. *Ormsby*. Bridge over Gill. James Pennyman.

1768. *Cold Kirby*. Admission of Sir James Pennyman.

1667—71. *Stainton*. Sir James Pennyman.

1610. *Thornton*. James Pennyman.

1615. Aug. 24. James Pennyman and others to Wm. Pennyman. Feoffment of part of the Manor of *Ormsby*.

1680. Sir Thos. Pennyman to Sir Wm. Hustler.

1722. *Great Stainton*, Durham. Sir James Pennyman and Sir Wm. Hustler.

1722. July 14. James Pennyman, 1st pt., Wm. Churchill and another, 2nd pt., William, Archbishop of Canterbury, and others, 3rd pt. Grant of annuity of £100 in trust for the intended wife of Sir James Pennyman.

1726. Settlement of one-third part of the Estate of Michael Warton.

1677. Sir James Pennyman and Thos. Pennyman. Conveyance of land in *Liverton*, etc. (not exemted).

21 James 1. James Pennyman, *Ormsby*.

1682—91. John Pennyman.

1722. Settlement on marre of Sir James Pennyman with Dorothy Wake.

1734. James Pennyman. *Ormsby Charity*.

HAILSTONE MSS. Box 4, 37.

4. 1670—1770. ABSTRACT OF TITLE of Sir James Pennyman bart., to a messuage situate in Fleinsop, par. Coverham, New Close, Three Midge Dales, Manny Close, East Closes, East Ings, Hull Dale, Low Bank, and Banks, in Fleinsop aforesaid, and 8 cattlegates in

Carleton pasture, purchased by Sir James Pennyman, grandfather of the said Sir James Pennyman, from John Nottingham, and also 3 messuages in Fleinsop, called West Fall, West Close, Broad Ing, Gutter Piece, Gill Heads, Stone Dales, Rasgill Close, and High East Close, all in Fleinsop, and 8 beastgates in Fleinsop Rough Pasture or Fleinsop Grain, and 3 beastgates in Carleton, purchased by the said Sir James, the grandfather, from Jonathan Ryder, and which upon his death descended to his eldest son Sir William Pennyman bart., deceased, and were afterwards purchased of him by Thomas Pennyman, 3rd son of the said Sir James, the grandfather, with part of the personal estate of the said Sir James, the grandfather, directed to be laid out in the purchase of lands to be settled to the uses of his will.

The abstract commences with several deeds of 21 Charles 2, conveying the estate (which had been vested in Commissioners for the Corporation of London for selling the Manors of Middleham and Richmond under letters patent of 4 Charles 1) to John Bartlett, junr., Alderman of Richmond, co. York.

In 1702, Bartlett conveyed to Wm. Horner, of Gammersgill, co. York, yeom., who in 1723 conveyed to John Nottingham, of Newstead, co. York, gent.

In 1738, Nottingham conveyed to Sir James Pennyman, the grandfather.

Then follows Probate of the will of Sir James Pennyman, bart., in 1745, as in appendix C. with a pedigree, shewing the decent of the property.

In 1746, Sir James Pennyman, of Thornton, bart., eldest son of Sir James, the grandfather, conveyed the estate to his brother Thomas, of Middleham, esqr., and a trustee, to the use of the said Thomas in tail male, with remainder to his brothers Warton Warton and Ralph Pennyman successively in tail male, with remainder to the right heirs of the said Sir James, the grandfather.

In 1770, the estate was conveyed by the Trustees to Sir James Pennyman, of Ormesby, bart., only son of Ralph Pennyman, late of Beverley, esqre., deceased, who was youngest son of Sir James Pennyman, of Thornton, co. York, bart., deceased, the said first named Sir James Pennyman being the only heir male living of any of the five sons of the said Sir James Pennyman. And in Easter term, 10 Geo. 3, a common recovery of the premises was suffered.

The above premises were probably only a part of much larger estates, for the abstract is marked "Lot 13," and in 1770 Sir James sold the estate by auction to one Wm. Humphrey, of Wensley, but unfortunately his solicitor described Fleinsop as a manor, whereas it was really only parcel of the manor of Carleton, so that the purchase had to be cancelled. With the abstract are a number of very curious letters on the subject, but they are thought to be much too long for insertion here.

Gc
92
P:
18

Go
92
P3
18

APPENDIX F.

EXTRACTS FROM THE YORKSHIRE FEET OF FINES.

2. A short explanation of these records may possibly be useful to some readers. A fine was an acknowledgment, in a Court of record, of a feoffment or conveyance of lands. It was usually described as an amicable agreement of a suit, either actual or fictitious, by leave of the king or his justices; whereby the lands in question became, or were acknowledged to be, the right of one of the parties. Originally it was founded on an actual suit, commenced at law for recovery of land; and the possession thus gained was found to be so sure and effectual, that fictitious actions came into ordinary use in the conveyance of land, for the sake of obtaining the same security. By an Act of 18 Ed. I, called "Modus levandi fines," these fictitious actions were recognised by law, and directions given for the manner of levying them. The party to whom the land was to be conveyed commenced an action at law against the person conveying. Then followed the *licentia concordandi*, or leave to agree the suit, for, as soon as the action was brought, the defendant, knowing himself to be in the wrong, was supposed to make overtures of peace to the plaintiff. And then came the *concord*, or fine itself, after leave obtained from the Court, by which the lands in question were acknowledged to be the right of the plaintiff. This was followed by the *note* of the fine, which was an abstract of the proceedings, naming the parties, the parcels of land, and the agreement. This was enrolled of record in the proper office, by direction of the Statute 5 Henry IV. c. 14, which is the reason why these records are still accessible to us in the Public Record Office. The final part was the *foot of the fine*, or conclusion of it; which recited the parties, date, and place, and before whom it was acknowledged or levied. Of this there were indentures made or engrossed, at the chirographer's office, and one delivered to each party, being written on one piece of parchment, cut in a curved line down the middle, so that when, even at the present day, the two parts can be brought

together again, they will be found to exactly fit into each other. The real reason for these fictitious conveyances or assurances of lands being winked at by the King's Courts would seem to be the very simple one, that at each stage of the proceedings, very substantial fees became due to the king.

The meaning of the following extracts from these Feet of Fines is this. The name of the purchaser of the land is given first, as the querent or plaintiff; then *v.* or *versus*; the name of the vendor, as defendant or deforciant; and lastly the description of the lands conveyed.

Hilary Term. 25 Eliz. (1582-3.)
James Pennyman, gent., *versus* Thos. Darcye and Colubra his wife. A third of the Manor of Murton, and of 4 messes and 4 cottages with lands in Murton and Ormsbye.

Mich. 27-28 Eliz. (1585.)
Ralph Crathorne esqr and James Pennyman, gent., *versus* James Strangwishe esqr. and Wm. Wilcoke. Messe with lands in East Upsall and West Upsall. The same *versus* James Strangwyshe esqr. and Robert Sturdye, gent. 6 messes and 3 cottages with lands in Tafford.

Hilary. 29 Eliz. (1586-7.)
James Pennyman gent. *versus* John Atherton esqr. and Katherine his wife. One third of the Manor of Murton alias Mororton and of 4 messes and 4 cottages with lands there and in Ormesbye.

Easter. 29 Eliz. (1587).
John Radclyffe gent., and James Pennyman gent., *versus* James Strangwayes esqr. and. Richd. Ablesonne. Messe with lands in East Upsall, near Ormesby, and in Cleveland, to be held by Richd. Ablesone for a term of 29 years next following the death of Matthew Pressidie.

Hilary. 30 Eliz. (1587-8.)
George Tocketts esqr. and James Pennyman *versus* John Atherton esqr. and Katherine his wife. 60 messes and 4 mills with lands in Mashe (Marske), and Uplethame.

Mich. 31-32 Eliz. (1589.)
James Pennyman gent. *versus* James Strangwayes esqr. Manors of afforcklias near Allerton, and Tanton alias Tampton near Stokesley, and 20 messes and 20 cottages with lands there and in Brotton.

Hilary. 35 Eliz. (1592-3.)

>Thomas Hutchison, Christopher Potter, and Emmotta Easbye *versus* James Pennyman and Ann his wife. Messuages and 3 cottages in Stokesley.

Trin. 38 Eliz. (1596.)

>Wm. Kyndersley one of the Cursitors of the Court of Chancery, and Martyn Smyth, gent., also a cursitor of the same Court *versus* James Pennyman, gent., and Ann his wife. Manor of Taunton alias Tampton, next Stokesley, and 12 messes and 12 cottages with lands there and in Newbie, Ayton, and Brotton.

Mich. 38-39 Eliz. (1596.)

Anthony Metcalfe, gent., and James Metcalfe, gent., *versus* Wm. Pennyman and Ann his wife, as to the same manor, and 3 messes and a cottage with lands there and in Ayton.

Mich. 39-40 Eliz. (1597.)

Robt. Trotter esqr. and Hy. Trotter *versus* Wm. Pennyman and Ann his wife. 10 messes and 10 cottages with lands in Brotton.

Trin. 40 Eliz. (1598.)

Samuel Brasse one of the clerks of Wm. Pennyman, one of the Cursitors of the Court of Chancery, *versus* Robt. Cowper esqr. and others. 2 messes with lands in Thorneton and Staynton.

Hilary. 41 Eliz. (1598-9.)

Wm. Pennyman, gent., a cursitor of the Court of Chancery *versus* Wm. Megotson, gent. 3 messes with lands in Normanby.

Trinity. 41 Eliz. (1599.)

Geo. Stowpe *versus* Wm. Pennyman esqr. and Ann his wife. Messe with lands in Brotton.

Mich. 42-43 Eliz. (1600.)

James Pennyman, gent., *versus* Ralph Rookebye, gent., and Joan his wife. Manor of Ormesbye and 10 messes, 5 cottages, a water mill, and a windmill with lands in Ormesbye, Caldecotes, and South Cowton.

Easter. 44 Eliz. (1602.)

John Harte, knt., Edwd. Cage senr. and Judith his wife, and Geo. Bolles senr. and Joan his wife *versus* Strangwaies Bradshawe esqr. and Elizabeth his wife, and James Pennyman, gent., and Ann his wife. The Manors of Sneton and Murton alias Mororton and 14 messes, 4 cottages, and 2 mills with lands in the same and in Whitbie and Ormsbye.

APPENDIX F.

Mich[s]. 44-45 Eliz. (1602.).

James Pennyman, gent., *versus* Francis Fryster and James Fryster. Messes with lands in Catwicke and Sneton.

Same term. James Pennyman, senr., gent., *versus* Christ. Bulmer, gent., and Margaret his wife. 3 messes and 2 cottages with lands in Ormesbye and Caldcoates.

Note.—As to the surname of Kindersley given above in this Appendix, and in the first entry in the Ormesby Parish Register extracts in 1603, given in appendix B., p. 13

It seems difficult to determine whether the name of James Pennyman's wife, whom he married at Ormesby in 1603, was really Kindersley or Kingsley. The facts are these—

1 In the marriage entry in the Ormesby Parish Register, it is spelt Kindersley.

2 An entry in the Feet of Fines for 1596 states that William Kyndersley, one of the Cursitors of the Court of Chancery, and Martyn Smyth, gent., also a Cursitor of the same Court, levy a fine against James Pennyman, gent., and Ann his wife, as to the Manor of Tampton next Stokesley, and lands there and elsewhere. [See above.]

3 An entry in a Schedule of Deeds formerly belonging to Lady Pennyman, in which a deed occurs, dated Aug 31, 1603, between James Pennyman of the first part, William Kyndersley of the second part, and James Pennyman, son of the said James Pennyman and another of the third part, being a settlement of lands in Ormesby on the marriage of James Pennyman the son with Catherine Kyndersley. [See appendix E., p. 48.]

3 In the Report of 12 Nov. 1647 in the Royalist Composition Paper, the name is spelt Kindesley (not Kindersley) all through. [See appendix J., p. 85.]

On the other hand Mr. Pennyman has the following short pedigree, in the handwriting of the late Rev. C. B. Norcliffe, without any reference to the authority from which it was taken —

WILLIAM KINGSLEY of Chorley co. Lanc. = DAMARIS dau of John Abbot of
(Vert, a cross engrailed ermine, in the   Guidford. brother to George.
first quarter a mullet cr.)   Archbp. of Canterbury.

WILLIAM KINGSLEY, D.D., Archdeacon of
Canterbury, Fellow of All Souls',
Oxford, ob. Jan. 29, 1647 had 16
children.

Another short pedigree, in Mr. Pennyman's possession, is as follows —

GULIELMUS KINSLEY DE CHORLEY = KATHARINE TOTHILL.
co. Lanc et de Rosehall co. Hertf.   ob. 1622, aged 74. Buried
ob, 1611. Buried at Sarret in Herts.   in Canterbury Cathedral.

KATHERINE uxor Jacobi Pennyman de
Ormesby arm. pata Domini Jacobi
Pennyman militis et Baronetti. Ille
obiit 1655.

Glover's Visitation of Yorkshire, 1612 (Edited by Joseph Foster, 1875), says that James Pennyman married the " dau of . . . . Kingsley.

Dugdale's Visitation, 1665, says " Cath. da of Willm. Kingsley of Canterbury."

In the Royalist Composition Papers, also, under date 28 Oct. 1647, are the entries as to an annuity payable to William Kingsley, D.D., of Canterbury, by reason of a grant made to his father William Kingsley esq, and another as to annuity to Mrs. Kingsley. [See appendix J., p 84.]

The will of James Pennyman, dated 1655, also mentions his brother Kingsley. [See appendix C. No 7, p, 27.]

Gc
92
P3
18

APPENDIX G.

INQUISITIONS POST MORTEM.

1. [Chancery Inquisitions post mortem. Series II., Vol. 515, No. 80.]

    Inquisition taken at Stokesley, co. York, after the death of James Pennyman, late of Stokesley, esquire.

    27 Sept.: 1 Charles I. (Writ dated 30 May: 1 Charles I.)

    He was seised of a moiety of the manor or house of Ormesbie and Caldcotes, co. York, and lands, &c., there, held of Sir Thomas Bellasis, bart., and Katherine Atherton, widow, by tenure to the jury unknown. Also of a messuage and 2 acres of pasture in Stokesley, which he bequeathed to James Sarton, son of Allan Sarton; held of Richard Foster, esquire, as of his Manor of Stokesley. He died 29 Nov. last. James Pennyman, esquire, his son and heir, was then aged 45.

2. [Chancery Inquisitions post mortem. Series II., Vol. 444, No. 84.]

    Inquisition taken at Stokesley, co. York, upon the death of William Penniman, esquire, formerly one of the six clerks of the High Court of Chancery.

    3 Sept.: 4 Charles I. (Writ dated 27 May: 4 Charles I.)

    The deceased was seised of one-third of the manor (*sic*) of Marske, Upleatham, and Ridcarr, co. York, with pasture for cattle on Skelton More, all lately belonging to Lord Conyers, deceased; and other tenements in Marske, Easby, &c., and of the site of the Grange or capital messuage of the Manor of Marske, and twelve boon-days belonging to the manor aforesaid; the rectory of Marske, and all tithes of fish at Ridcarr; tenements in Brotton bought of John Marley, gent., and William Hall; a messuage in *Ormsby (in Upsalls in that parish), and a moiety of the Manor of Ormsby; and tenements in Ormsby and Caldcotes, formerly parcel of the hereditaments of James Strangwaies, esquire, deceased; and of a moiety of

---

* Ormsby is spelt *Ornsby* throughout.

one other Manor of Ormsby, late purchased of Queen Elizabeth; and of a capital messuage tenements in St. Albones, co. Hertford.

By his will, dated 24 Feb. 1625-6, he bequeathed his lands to his brother Mr. James Pennyman, of Ormsby, esquire, and his cousin Mr. James Morley, esquire, upon trust to pay his debts; to his wife Anne, for life, lands in Caldcoates, &c., with remainder to his son William. He died 28 April, 4 Charles I. William Pennyman, ... * his son and heir, then aged 19. His wife Anne is still living.

3. [Chancery Inquisitions post mortem. Series II., Vol. 535, No. 69.]

Inquisition taken at Stoxley, co. York, after the death of Dame Anne Pennyman, late the relict of Sir William Pennyman, knight, deceased.　　　　　12 April, 1658. (Writ dated 18 Dec., 1657.)

The said Anne was seised of one-third of the Manor of Skelton of the yearly value of 90^{li} and lands in Stanghen and Hinderwell; one-third of the Manor of Eston, of the yearly value of 108^{li}; and the liberty of Langbarugh, with wreck of the sea, and anchorage and groundage of ships in the river Tease; and waifs and strays, &c., &c., upon the skarres betwixt Yarmebridge and Runswick, in right of the said liberty, and seaweed driven ashore there, which seaweed since the death of the said Anne was, for the use of Conyers Darcy, Lord Darcy and Conyers, as heir to the said Dame Anne, demised for a certain rent.

She did in her lifetime acknowledge the said Conyers Darcy to be her heir when she should die.

Dame Anne had also a right of inheritance to a burgage in Northallerton, and certain lands in Skipton Bridge and Thornton Steward, but the quality and quantity thereof the jury know not. She died in or about June 1644.

The said Lord Darcy and Conyers, of Hornbie Castle, is her cousin and next heir, and was aged at the death of the said Anne about 45.

N.B.—There are no other Pennyman Inquisitions post mortem between the reign of Hen. 7 and Charles 2.

*Almost illegible here.

APPENDIX H.

DESCENT OF THE MANOR OF ORMESBY.

Translation of a MS. apparently compiled in the 16th century, now in possession of Mr. J. Munby, York.

Kildale. A brief descent of the Percies and Strangwayes, from Mr. James Pennyman, who claims Ormesby and other estates by reason of a marriage between Strangways Bradshaw, cousin and heir of James Strangewayes, esqr., lately deceased, of the one part, and the daughter of the said James Pennyman of the other part.

13 Edward 1. Alexander Percy gave his Manors of Ormesby, Upsall, and Caldecott, to Wm. Percy, his son, and his heirs for ever.

The said William died seised of the manors in fee simple, and his son and heir was Arnold de Percy.

Arnold de Percy gave the Manors of Ormesby, Caldecott, Upsall, and other estates to his brother William de Percy and his heirs.

The said William de Percy gave the same to his son Wm. Percy in tail, with remainder to him and his heirs for ever.

The said William Percy had a daughter Julia, who married Robt. Conyers, and had all the said lands by ancient indenture from said William, her father, the trustees being Francis Conyers, John de Martin, and Richard de Welton.

The said Trustees granted all the said lands in Upsall, Whitby Strand, Ormesby, Caldecott, Cauthorn, and Tampton, to said Robt. Conyers and Julia ux. in tail, with reversion to John Conyers in tail, with remainder to the heirs of the body of said Robert Conyers, with remainder to his right heirs.

The said Robert and Julia ux. had a son Robert Conyers, junr.

The said Robert, the son, had a son and heir Robt. Conyers, who had a daughter Anne, who married James Strangways, of Harlesay, and had a son James Strangways.

The said James Strangways had a son Richard Strangways, who had a son James Strangways, now his only child, who had an only daughter married to one Crathorne, of Crathorne, and she had issue, dead it is said. (1598.)

Inquisition post mortem, 4 Aug.: 5 & 6 Philip and Mary.

The jury say that Richard Strangwayes died seised in fee of the Manor of Ormesby in Cleveland, and of the Manor of Caldcots, and of a messuage, etc., in West Upsall, etc., and a messuage, etc., and two water-mills in East Upsall. And that the Manors of Ormesby and Caldcots were held of the King and Queen by reason of the minority of the heir of Sir John Conyers, kt., Lord Conyers, lately deceased, as of his Manor of Yeorome, in Socage, and are worth beyond reprisals £30, and the rest held of the same and are worth, etc., £13.

Kildale Manor. Md. yt apperit by diverse Auncyent Endentures yt Ormesby, Craythorn, Caldcots, Upsall, Nunthorpe, Ayrsome, Barwick, Thormanby, Lasingby, and Normanby, were parcel of the Manor of Kyldale, and holden of the Lord of the said manor by Knight Service, 13 Ed. 1.

Anno. 13 Ed. 1. Upsall was the land of Arnold de Percy, and Ormesby and Caldcote of the said Alexander. Alexander de Percy had a son John as is contained in an Inquisition taken on the death of Arnold de Percy, a$^{o.}$ 17 Ed. 2, and he had £4 land in Crathorne. And by another deed of John, son of Stephen le Tewler, a$^{o.}$ 3 Ed. 2, that Alexander held his lands in Ormesby, of Arnold Percy, kt., lord of Kildale.

Mem. 7 Henry 4. Ralph Bulmer died seised of the Manors of Ormesby, Upsall, Welton, and other estates.

EXTRACTED FROM GLOVER'S & DUGDALE'S VISITATIONS.

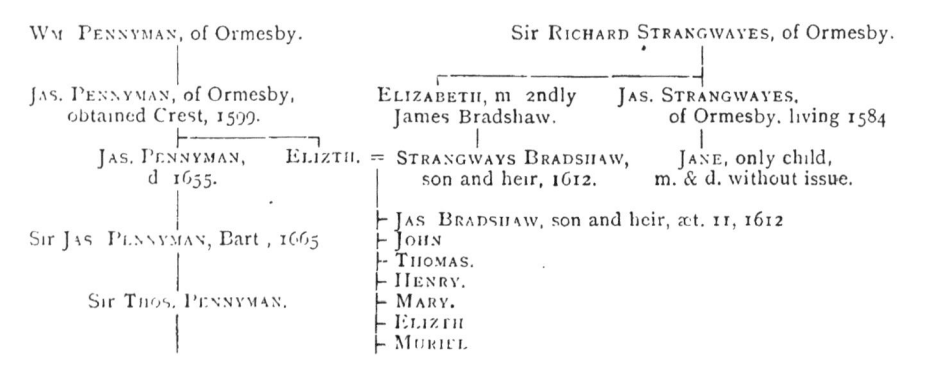

WM PENNYMAN, of Ormesby.
|
JAS. PENNYMAN, of Ormesby,
obtained Crest, 1599.
|
JAS. PENNYMAN, ELIZTH. =
d 1655.
|
Sir JAS PENNYMAN, Bart , 1665
|
Sir THOS. PENNYMAN.

Sir RICHARD STRANGWAYES, of Ormesby.
|
ELIZABETH, m 2ndly   JAS. STRANGWAYES,
James Bradshaw.   of Ormesby. living 1584
| |
STRANGWAYS BRADSHAW,   JANE, only child,
son and heir, 1612.   m. & d. without issue.

├ JAS BRADSHAW, son and heir, æt. 11, 1612
├ JOHN
├ THOMAS.
├ HENRY.
├ MARY.
├ ELIZTH
├ MURIEL

APPENDIX I.

GRANT OF A CREST TO HIS ANCIENT ARMS, TO JAMES PENNYMAN IN 1599.

Translation of the Grant of a Crest to James Pennyman, Esq., in 1599.

To all and singular to whom this present writing shall come to be seen William Segar esquire called Norroy King of Arms and Principal Herald of the North Parts of the Kingdom of England (sends) Greeting —Whereas James Pennyman of Ormesbye in the County of York son and heir of William Pennyman of Murton* in the County aforesaid Esquire deceased, son and heir of Robert Pennyman Esquire, on account of his love towards his paternal family has besought me that I would describe and assign to him some Crest as it is called for an ornament and ensign upon his helmet or head-piece to be placed above his shield or family coat of arms and insignia which has been worn and used by the ancestors of his family from old time, which both he himself and his descendants may be able lawfully and without prejudice to anyone to use and enjoy. Now I, being not only ready to perform that which pertains to my office in this behalf, but also desirous to gratify a man famous for his valour and many other titles as well as deserving well of the State, have caused to be declared in French words according to heraldic custom the ancestral and proper arms or insignia of his family as they have heretofore been used by his ancestors, together with a crest to be placed upon his helmet, and for a fuller knowledge of the same I have taken care to have them delineated in the margin of these presents in their metals and colours according to custom. Videlicet. Gules a chevron Ermine between three steels or butts of broken spears proper And further in decoration of his helmet to which the said shield appends I have assigned to him for a Crest as follows—A Helmet: out of a Mural Crown, a Lion's head erased Or wounded and pierced through the neck with a broken spear, "mantee" Gules, "double" Argent. Which ancestral arms and insignia worn and used by his progenitors, together

---

*Murton means Morton, a township in the parish of Ormesby. In 1822 it contained only 3 farm-houses, and 26 inhabitants.

with the said Crest placed upon his helmet and with all the rest of the appendages and ornaments as more clearly to be seen depicted in the margin, I the aforenamed Norroy by virtue and authority of my office have granted and ratified and by these presents have confirmed and approved to the aforesaid James Pennyman and his issue and to all persons descending from him for ever. So that it shall be lawful for the said James and his posterity to have and to hold the said Arms and Crest and the other ornaments as they are above described and declared as their family insignia and proper to their family and the same at all places and times to show on shields, bucklers, targets, banners, rings or robes, or in any other lawful manner at their will and pleasure and to use and enjoy the same as ensigns for ever, any contradiction of any person whomsoever to the contrary notwithstanding. In Faith and Testimony of all which things I the aforesaid Norroy have subscribed my own hand to these presents and by the appension of the seal of my aforesaid office have corroborated this present writing. Dated at London in the Office of Arms 10 May Anno Domini 1599.

Will: Segar, King of Arms.

APPENDIX J.

ROYALIST COMPOSITION PAPERS,

OR THE PROCEEDINGS OF THE COMMITTEE FOR COMPOUNDING WITH DELINQUENTS DURING THE COMMONWEALTH.

(Extracted from the Composition Papers preserved in the Public Record Office.)

Cases against Sir James Pennyman, and James Pennyman, Esq., his father, of Ormesby and Marske, for opposing the Landing of Cromwell's soldiers at Marske, from the Rainbow and other ships, in the Summer of 1643; and against Sir William Pennyman, bart., and William Pennyman, of Gray's Inn.

It may be useful to give here the following extracts from the Introduction to the Royalist Composition Papers for Yorkshire, edited by J. W. Clay, Esq., F.S.A. This appendix includes several Pennyman papers from the original records, not in that volume.

It appears that in 1644, the Parliament being much in want of money for payment of the Scottish army and for other purposes, conceived the idea of making the Royalists, or Delinquents, as it called them, compound for their estates, and a Committee that had been formed at Goldsmiths' Hall for the finding of money for the service of the State came to have the management of this scheme.

In July and August, 1644, the compounding began, but only with such people as had been previously sequestered, and it was not till March, 1645, that the Committee had authority from the House of Commons to compound with any who should tender themselves, or to summon whom it thought fit. On August 12 it was ordered that estates were to be compounded for at two years' estimated value before the war. This arrangement seems to have been carried out in most of the compositions, in addition to a fine of a tenth part of the value of goods and chattels. Those persons who were not worth £200 seem to have escaped..............

The Composition Papers are contained in about 269 volumes..............

The following is the course the unfortunate compounder had to pursue in making his composition, and the order of the papers.

He had first to get leave from the Committee to compound: when it was granted, he had to send up his petition with the particulars of his estate and certificates of his having taken the National Covenant before some approved Minister, and of his having signed the Negative Oath.

The officials then prepared a report of the nature of his delinquency, of their valuation of his property, and what amount they considered the fine ought to be.

All these papers having gone before the Committee at Goldsmiths' Hall, it then proceeded to name the fine, which was written at the end of the report and duly entered in the minute book. Sometimes there are additional affidavits, letters, and certificates from the County Committee and other officials.

The compounder had generally to pay a moiety of his fine at once, time being given to him for the remainder. If he failed to pay in time, which seems not unfrequently to have happened, he was threatened with a resequestration of his estate.

The following papers have been, for the most part, arranged by Mr. Pennyman in chronological order (many of them by internal evidence only), but the Report on the cases of Sir James Pennyman, and his father James Pennyman esqr., is given first, because it gives a general view of the whole of the circumstances. Mr. Pennyman has also inserted the headings in brackets, in order to present to his readers a complete picture of the proceedings, and to give everything of interest in full, whilst avoiding tedious repetitions.

REPORT UPON THE CASE OF SIR JAMES PENYMAN OF ORMESBY.
G. 179, p. 1.

Sir James Pennyman† of Ornesby in the Countye of Yorke knt. and James Penyman* of the same place and County Esq. father to the said Sir James.

The Delinquency of James Pennyman the father aged 68 yeeres as is certified by the Committee in Yorke, is for executing the Commission of Array and that he did array men at Stoxly January 28th 1643, and did other like acts against the Parliament friends, and was in Armes alsoe, that he for a time refused to take the Couenant, and disputed against it both by word and wrightinge, that all his sonnes have bin engaged in the King's service.

Sir James his delinquency that he was in Armes against the Parliament a Colonell on the Kings side, but laid downe his Armes two yeeres sithence and had a passe from the Committee of Yorke to pass into Holland whither he went and there contynued for seaven monthes till he returned backe to make his Composition.

The father petitioned here in November, and had a letter to the Committee of Yorke who did certify his estate and delinquency accordingly, and Sir James the 11th of March 1645 tooke the Solemne League and Covenant at Margaretts where he landed as is certified by the Officers there, and for more satisfaction hath now taken it here againe before William Barton Minister of John Zacharies the fourth of April 1646 and the Negative Oath here the 26th of March 1646.

That the father hath taken both the National Covenant and Negative Oath before the Committee at Yorke as they make returne, by their Certificate dated 28 of February 1645.

They compound upon a particular delivered in under both their hands and another returned by the Committee to which they have subscribed to submit to such fine &c. and by which it doth appeare

That James Pennyman the father is seized in fee to him and his beires in possession of and in certaine lands and tenements lyinge and beinge in Ormsby and Normanby in the County of Yorke of the cleere yearly value before theis troubles £319 6 8 for which his fine is £638 13 4.

†Sir James Pennyman was created a baronet by Charles II,, married Elizabeth, daughter of Stephen Norcliffe, and was buried at Ormesby, April 24, 1679. The baronetcy expired in 1852, when the estates came into the Worsley family.

*James Pennyman (the Father) married first Catherine, daughter of William Kindersley, or Kingsley, of Canterbury [See Note at end of appendix F.]   secondly, Joane, daughter of—Smith, and had a family by each wife. He was buried at Ormesby, October 19th, 1655, and his will is given in appendix C., p. 27.

That he is possessed of the remaine of a tearme of 16 yeeres yet to come of and in certaine tithes renneinge and cominge in the townes and fields of Ormsby aforesaid in the said County holden of the Bpp. of Yorke at the rent of £4 per an. and was of the yeerely value before theis troubles over and above the rent reserved £29 for which his fine is £40.

That he is seized of a ffrankten^te duringe the terme of two lives of other tythes lyinge in Marton* in the said County holden of the Arch Bpp. of Yorke at £8 per an. rent and was of the yeerely value before theis troubles over and above the rent reserved £78 for which his fine at a yeere and a quarter is £97 10 0.

That he is seized to him and the heires of his body in divers other messuages lands and tenements lying and being in Maske, Redcar and Upleatham in the said County and were Sir William Pennymans and his wifes, and granted by them to him, and the heires of his body about 14 yeeres since as the Committee doe certifye, and were of the yeerely value before theis troubles £600 for which his fine is £1200.

That Sir James Pennyman the sonne is seized in fee to him and his heires in possession of and in other lands and tents. lyinge and beinge in Ormsby aforesaid in the said County of the yeerely value before theis troubles £110 for which his fine is £220.

That they have compounded with the said Committee for their personal estate.

Their whole ffine doe amount to the somme of £1835 3 4.

   Jerom. Alexander.   Sam. Moye.

	£	s.	d.
The fine of the old man is	1750	0	0
Of which the Committee doth think fit to abate of £55 0 0 for £50 per an. to be settled on the Vicar of Maske ...	550	0	0
	1200	0	0
The young man's fine is	530	0	0
(Upon payment of the moiety, the £30 to be considered.)			
	£1730	0	0

£50 is to be settled upon ye Rectory of Gisbrough out of ye profitts of ye Rectory of Maske for which £500 is to be abated.

April 25, 1646. G 3, p. 86. 1646, Aug. 6. The fine was passed by the House of Commons Jas. Pennyman £1200, ditto the younger £537. G 1, p. 137.

  *Query, Morton, a township in the parish of Ormesby.—J.W.P.

(Sir James Pennyman takes the National Covenant and goes abroad.)

These are to certifie that Sir James Pennyman of Ormesby in the county of York knight did freely and fully take the National Covenant and subscribe the same. Upon the fourth day of Aprill 1645. The said Covenant being administered unto him according to order by me.

WILLIAM BURTON,
Minister of John Zecharies
London.

G. 179, p. 23.

By the Comittee of the Warre at York xix of Sept 1645. These are to require euerie of you to permit and suffer Sr James Pennyman Knight with his servants their horses & necessaryes for their iourney to pass unto Kingston upon Hull or Scarborough and from thence to pass by ye first conveniency of shipping into Holland wthout any lett or molestation   Provided they carry nothing of danger or prejudicall to ye State.

Math Boynton.   George Trotter.   ffran Pierpont.
Wm. Allanson.   J. Alured.

(The next and many other papers, of which no explanation is given, tell their own story.)

PETITION OF SIR JAMES PENNYMAN, OF ORMESBY, CO. YORK.

G. 179, p. 15.

To the Honoble the Committee for Compositions
sitting at Goldsmiths Hall.

The humble Petition of Sir James Pennyman, of Ormesby,
in the county of York, knt.

Sheweth:

That your Petitioner having formerly served as Collonell in the kings army did about two years since lay downe his commission and afterwards did quitt the kings quarters & repair to his owne home & having procured a passe from the Committee for the Parliament resideing at York for his safe convoy into Holland did accordingly resort thither, where he hath contynued these seaven monthes last past. And being now further desirous to give a more ample testimony of his obedience unto the Parliament hath made his returne hither.

Hee therefore most humbly prayeth that hee may be admitted to compound for his estate, so as his wife and children may be able to subsist, the true value whereof he is reddy to present unto this Hob[le] Committee. As also that your Petitioner may be admitted to prosecute the Composition of James Pennyman Esq. the Petitioners father who is aged 70 years or thereabouts, and unfitt for travel, & whose estate & delinquency is already certifyed to this table from the Committee of York. And as he stands obliged shall ever pray, &c.

JAMES PENNYMAN.

Petition of James Pennyman, of Ormesby, co. York, Esq.

To the right hon. the Committee of Lords and Commons for an advance of Money.

The humble petition of James Pennyman, senior, of Ormsby, in the county of York, Esquier.

Sheweth :

That your petitioner being summoned to appeare before your Honours the 3d day of August instant for satisfying his twentieth part was and is ready to obey the same, but that by reason of his great age & many infirmities of his body and the far remoteness of his habitation from the Citie of London he is not able to attend this hono[ble] Committee without the great hazard of his life.

That he hath already satisfied his said 20th part to the Committee in the Country and there compounded and paid for his personal estate and is very much indebted.

Therefore humbly prayeth that your Honours would be pleased to grant him two months tyme his dwelling being 200 miles distant to the end he may procure the certificates of the Committee in the county for what he hath already paid and may make oath there (he being not able to travel to London) of all his just debts, soe that his case may be made cleere to yo[r] Honors and your Petitioner receive justice therein.

For which as in duty bound he shall ever pray, &c.

(James and Sir James Pennyman give particulars of their estates for the purpose of determining the "twentieth part," the fine which they have to pay before they can get leave to compound.)

The case of James Pennyman, Esq.

	£	s.	d.
He compounds at Goldsmiths Hall for c'teyne lands in Ormsby for life worth per an. £188 6 8 which at 7 years purchase is	1316	0	0
He is seized in fee of c'teyne lands in Normanby in the said county of York per an. £130 which at 15 years is ...	1950	0	0
He hath tythes in Normanby aforesaid held by lease for 16 yeares worth declared £29 per an. which at 6 years is...	174	0	0
He hath tythes at Marton in Com. Yorke held for two lives of the Bpp. of Yorke per an. £78 which at 8 years purchase is	624	0	0
	4064	0	0
He compounds also for the reversion of his lands in Ormsby after his (fathers) death of the value of £130 which will amount to	1040	0	0
	5104	0	0
He likewise compounds for an estate of £600 per an. of Sir William Pennyman who was indebted £20,000 as per his particular which at 15 years is	9000	0	0
	£14104	0	0

	£	s.	d.
He craves a deduction for £10,040 debts owing by him and Sir Wm. Pennyman	10040	0	0
As also of £100 per an. to the Vicar of Marske and Gisborough for ever which comes to £1500...	1500	0	0
Also to Tho. Ruddock during his life per an. £20 which at 7 yeares purchase is...	140	0	0
To Mrs. Kingsley £50 which is	400	0	0
	£12080	0	0

So that £12,080 being deducted out of £14,104 the rest is £2,024 the 20th part of which is £101 4 0.

G. 179. p. 11.

A particular of the estate of James Pennyman, of Ormsby, in the county of Yorke.

He hath lands in Ormsby for life whereof he is seised worth in the best tymes per an.	188	6	8
He hath lands in Normanby in the said county whereof he is seised in fee which was worth in the best tymes per an.	130	0	0
He hath tythes in Normanby aforesaid which he holds by lease from the Bpp. of York for 16 yeares yet to come worth yearly (besides £4 rent payable to the Bpp. for the same	29	0	0
He hath other tythes in Marton in the said county of York which he holds by lease from the said Bpp. of Yorke for 2 lives yett lyving worth yearely besides viij^h rent payable to the Bpp. for the same	78	0	0
Suma. tot' £426	6	8

He hath already compounded for his personal estate as by the Certificate from the Committee at York appeareth. £176.

He hath likewise an estate of inheritance of all the lands and tythes in Maske Redcar and Upleatham, which were Sir William Pennymans & his Lady granted unto the heires of his body by Joane his now wife. For which he cannot for the present compound by reason that the Lord Darcy & others doe challenge a title therein as heires at law. And for that the debts of the said Sir William Pennyman doe exceed the some of twenty thousand pounds which lands are desired to be continued in sequestration & are worth yearly £600.

JAMES PENNYMAN.

Vera Copia exd., Jo. Leech.

G. 179, p. 14.

Particular of the estate of Sir James Pennyman, of Ormesby in the county of York knt. as it hath been lett at the rack in the best tymes.

He hath lands in Ormesby whereof he is seised in fee worth in the best tymes cx^{li}.

He hath the revercon of lands in Ormsby after the death of his ffather & Mother worth per an. cxxxviii^h vi^s viii^d as it is certyfied by the Committee. As for his personal estate he hath not any.

JAMES PENNYMAN.

Vera copia ex.
Jo. Leech.

```
          1650
          1104
          ————
          2754  estate.
           700  debts.
          ————
  £102.   2054...20th part.
```

24 October, 1645.

William Burnett of Staple Inn gent. appeared for James Pennyman of Ormesby in Com. Yorke, who hee affirms is not able to come in person. Therefore a letter to be written to the Committee &c. & take ye oath & whether he bee not able to attend as is pretended.

G. 179, p. 19.

Letter from the Committee at York to the Commissioners at London.

Honble

In answer to your letter we have informed ourselves of the crymes & estate of James Penyman of Ormesby in the Northriding of the Countye of Yorke Esq. (being aged sixtie eight years) & doe certifie that he was a Commissioner of Array and did array men at Stoxley, January 28th 1643 & two other times their and once at Gisbrough. That in February 1644 by direction from Mr. John Bellasis hee with Mr. Bradshaw did proportion & mitigate the fines sett upon several men in Cleveland by the said governor of Yorke. That in somer 1643 hee with some others of the country assembled with such armes as they had to hinder & oppose the seamen from coming ashore at Maske from aboard the Rainbow and other shippes. That in May 1644 hee absented himself from his house for fear of the Parliaments forces; that when the Covenant was tendered him by a Minister at his owne Church, hee refused to take it and disputed both by word and writeinge against it. That all his sonnes have been engaged in the Kings service (vizt) his eldest sonne Sir James a Coll. his second sonne Mr. William Penyman a Captaine, his third sonne Mr. Thomas Penyman late parson of Stoxley fled from thence when the Parliaments forces came, and his youngest sonne was longe in the South with his brother Coll. Sir James Penyman and Capt. Will. Penyman. For his estate it is certaine lands in Ormesby dureing his natural life the remainder to his said sonne Sir James Penyman, letten at racke in the best tymes at the rent of one hundreth eightie eight pounds six shillings eight pence per an. now worth yearly one hundreth fiftie pounds. That he hath an estate of all the lands in Maske Redcar & Upleatham which were Sir Will. Penyman and his wives granted by them to him and the beires of his body, about fourteene yeares since by fine letten in the best tymes as wee are informed at the racke rent of about six hundreth pounds per an. now worth yearly five hundreth pounds; That he hath an estate of lands in Normanby to himselfe & Joan & his heirs begotten of the body of the said Joan & for default of such issue to the right heirs of him for ever & letten in the best tymes for one hundreth thirtie one pounds per an. now worth one hundreth pounds yearly. That he hath a lease of Tith in the said Normanby which determines in the year 1662, under the yearly rent of four pounds to the Bishope letten at racke in the best tymes for thirtie three pounds per an. now lett yearly for two and twentie pounds. That he hath a lease of a Tith in Marton for two lives under the Bishop of Eight pounds per an. letten in the best tymes at the racke for eightie six pounds per an. now worth yearely Seaventy pounds per an.

That he hath a personal estate of two hundreth thirtie nine pounds twelve shillings of which was allowed his wife a fifth part and he paid the other four parts one hundreth seaventy six pounds. That he hath now taken the National Covenant & the oath of the fifth of April last all which wee humbly certifie and rest.

Your affectionate and humble servants,

To. Bourchier, Vic.
Rich. Darley.
Bar. Bouchier.
Robt. Walter.
Matthew Beckwith.
Chr. Perechay.

Yorke, 28 February,
    1646.

Addressed:
    ffor the Hono[ble] the Committee at Goldsmiths Hall.

G. 179, p. 31.

Whereas Sir James Penniman knt. hath shewed me a passport from Sir Mathew Bointon George Trotter, and Mr. Perpoint Sir William Allingson & Mr. Allured to pass into Holland where he hath bin for some time and is now desirous to go to London to compound there with ye Parliament of England I shall desir all officers by land and sea to suffer him quietly to pass provided he carry no letters or messuages dangerous to the state.

By me WALTER STRICKLAND imployed here by ye Parliament of England.

Hagh. March $\frac{3}{28}$ 1646.

To all officers in ye service of
ye Parliament of England
by land and sea.

G. 3, p. 86.   26 August, 1646.

ffynes past in the House of Commons.

James Pennyman £1200
James Pennyman the younger ... ... £ 537

G. 4, p. 131.   26 October, 1647.

Whereas James Pennyman of Ormesby in ye county of Yorke Esq. having bin formerly fyned for his delinquency £1750 which upon settling of £50 per an. for increase of mayntenance for a preaching minister in ye Church of Maske for ever was reduced to £1200 whereof six hundred pounds is already paid. It ls now further ordered that if ye said James Pennyman shall likewise settle £50 per an. for ever for an increase of mayntenance to ye Minister of Gisborough & his successors out of the profitts of ye Rectory of Maske aforesaid hee shall bee abated fyve hundred pounds in ye latter payment of his fine in lieu of the same.

(Mr. Pennyman now finds that he had omitted to deduct from the total annual value of his estate a rent charge of £50 in favour of his father-in-law, Dr. Kindersley or Kingsley, of Canterbury, and applies to have the error rectified.)

G. 179, p. 9. 26 October, 1647.

By the Commissioners for Compounding, &c.

Upon motion in the case of James Pennyman of Ormesby in ye county of York, Esq. It being alledged that there is a rent charge of £50 per an. issuing out of his estate which was not mentioned at ye time of his Composition. It is now ordered that it be referred to ye sub-Committee to examine the writings and proofes and consider of the truth of the same.

JO. LEECH.

G. 179, p. 5.

James Pennyman of the city of Dunelme knight maketh oath that to his knowledge for many years the some of fifty pounds being the moytye of an annual or yearly rent of one hundred pounds issueing out of the manor of Ormesbye & Caldicott in the county of York granted by James Pennyman this deponents grandfather & James Pennyman this deponents father hath been paid to Doctor Kingsley of Canterbury as due unto him by vertue of the grant aforesaid.

JAMES PENNYMAN.

Jurat 28 Octob. 1647.
Robt. Aylett.

G. 179, p. 8.

William Kingsley Dr. in Divinity of Canterbury maketh oath that for the space of seventeen years or thereabouts he hath received from James Pennyman Esquire of Ormesby in the county of York the yearly rent of fifty pounds by the yeare part of an annuity or rent charge out of the Manor of Ormesby and Caldicotts as by the writings more fully appeare. And that the foresaid summe by reason of a grant made to his father William Kingsley Esquire hath been paid to his knowledge without any Scruple unto his elder brother Thomas Kingsley dying without issue and himself now living for the space of six and thirty years and upwards according to covenants and agreements in writing expressed.

(Signed) WILLIAM KINGSLEY.

jurat 28 Octob. 1647.
Robt. Aylett.

G. 179, p. 3.
Report upon the Rent Charge.

According to your order of the 26 of October 1647 we have considered of the case of James Pennyman Esq. to us referred touching a Rent charge of £50 not mentioned in his Composition. And doe finde:

That a Rent charge of £100 per an. was granted by deed dated 28th of May 4to Jacobi by James Pennyman the elder & James Pennyman the younger unto William Pennyman of St. Albones Esq. & his heires, out of the Manor of Ormesby & lands in Caldicot in the **Countye** of Yorke.

That William Pennyman by his deed dated the 30th of November 8° Jacobi assigned the same rent charge to William Tothill Esquire & William Kindesley gent and their **heires**.

That one moiety of the said £100 per an. was purchased in by the Compounder.

That for the other moiety being £50 per an. the said Wm. Kindesley by his last will in writeing dated 1st of January 1611 & proved in the Prerogative Court of Canterbury did devise the same £50 per an. unto his sonne William Kindesley now Doctor in Divinity, and the heires males of his body the remainder to his owne right heires. And that after the death of the said William Tothill, William Drake Esq. deceased being his heire by his deed dated 9 November 8 Caroli granted the said Rent charge of £50 per an. to the said Doctor Kindesley & the heires males of his body.

And it appears by the affidavit of Doctor Kindesley and of Sir James Pennyman sonne of the Compounder that the said £50 per an. hath bin duly paid to the said Doctor Kindesley till these troubles.

And we doe not finde that the said £50 was mentioned either in the Compounders particular or the Certificate from Yorke, or any wayes mentioned in the Composition. The Manor of Ormesby being therein rated at £188 6 8 per an.

All which we humbly submit to consideration.

SAM MOYER.

12 Nov. 1647.
Jo. Readinge.

Certificate that Mr. Pennyman has settled £50 each on the Vicars of Marske and Gisbro, and abstracts of the deed securing the same.

(Addressed) To his honoured friends the Treasurers to the right Honble the Commissioners for Compounding with Delinquents sitting at Goldsmiths Hall.

Gent.

According to an order of the right hon^ble the Commissioners for compounding with Delinquents sitting at Goldsmiths Hall dated the 26th of October 1647 James Pennyman of Ormsby in the county of Yorke Esq. hath settled fifty pounds per an. upon the Minister of Maske for ever And fifty pounds per an. upon the Minister of Gisborough for ever for his and there better increase and augmentation of livelihood. All which at the instance of the said James Pennyman I humbly certifie and remaine.

    Gent,

    Your humble serv^t

Lincolnes Inn.   EDW. RICH.
 27 Feb. 1647.

James Pennyman of Ormesby in the said County Esq. By deed dated 26 Feb. Anno. Dni. 1647 hath settled the Rectory of Marske of the value of £100 per an. upon Sir Thomas Widdrington and others in trust for the Ministers of Marske and Gisborough for ever.

 Consideration £1000.
 Cov^t seized in fee and free from incumbrances.
 Cov^t of the value.
 Cov^t to make further assurance.

A Redemise by deed 27 Feb. pred habend for 2000 yeares Reddend £100 per ann. vizt 20 May et 10 Novr.

 Cov^t to pay the rent.
 A Noie pene of 20s. a weeke after 20 daies.
 A Reentry after 30 daies.

(Here comes the discharge of the Sequestration of James Pennyman. The subsequent proceedings relate to his son, Sir James Pennyman, and are not of sufficient interest to set out at length).

Discharge of the Sequestration.

Goldsmiths Hall, London.

By the Com^{is} for Compounding &c. May 21 1649.

Whereas James Pennyman of Ormesby in the Countye of Yorke Esq. hath paid in the summe of seaven hundred poundes in parte of his ffine of seaventeene hundred and fifty pounds and hath settled fifty pounds per an. upon ye minister of Maske and fifty pounds per an. upon the Minister of Gisborough for ever for which he is allowed one thousand and ffifty pounds and accepted in lieu of the remainder of his said ffine. It is therefore Ordered that Mr. Wareing & Mr. Herring Treasurers doe forthwith upon sight hereof deliver up unto the said James Pennyman or William Pennyman his sonne his bond to be cancelled and for soe doing this shall be their warrant.

Art. Hastings.	John Ashe.
D. Watkins.	Sam. Moye.
Joh. Dove.	D. Watkins.
G. ffenwick.	Richard Vennar.

A particular of the debts due & oweing by Sir James Pennyman of Ormesbie in the County of York knight.

Imprimis unto Nicholas Pearson £260 principal money by bond.
Item unto Mr. Swale £300 principal money by bond.

A particular of what debts he hath paid since his composition at Goldsmiths Hall.

Paid unto Mr. Pearson	£60
Paid unto Mr. Swale	£80

Sir James Pennyman of Ormesbie in the County of York, knight maketh oath that the list or particular of debts above written mentioned to be owing by this deponent are truly owing by this deponent and are just debts. And also that the several sums of money above mentioned to be paid by this deponent have been by this deponent and his assignes really paid since his composition at Goldsmiths Hall.

(Signed) JAMES PENNYMAN

John Page.　　　　　　　　　　　　　Jur. 7 die September 1649.

APPENDIX J.

A Particular of the debts due and oweinge by James Pennyman of Ormsby in the county of York Esquire.

	£	s.	d.
Imprimis. he is indebted to Sir Gervase Elwes of London knt. ...	4430	8	0
To Mr. Robert Lowther	1200	0	0
To the Contractors for the Allomes	500	0	0
To Mr. Williams	500	0	0
To Nicholas Pearson	450	0	0
To Jeffery Simpson	240	0	0
To Mr. Fourd	124	0	0
To Mrs. Peighen	124	0	0
To Mr. Roger Smith	220	0	0
To Sir John Gibson	1500	0	0
To John Allan	50	0	0
To Mr. Morton	120	0	0
To Mr. Wynne	116	0	0
To Richard Wilson Maryner	116	0	0
To Mr. Wildon	50	0	0
To Mr. Clark	100	0	0
To Mrs. Reeves	200	0	0

A Particular of what debts he hath paid since his Composition at Goldsmiths Hall.

	£	s.	d.
To Mrs. Goddard paid since his said Composition	£600	0	0
To Sir Gervase Elwes since his said Composition	700	0	0
To James Man of Ormesby	23	0	0

Sir James Pennyman of Ormsby in the county of York, knt. maketh oath that the list or particular of debts and sumes of money above mentioned to be owing by the above named James **Pennyman Esq.** (this deponents father) are truly owing by the said James Pennyman Esq. and are just debts. And also that the several sumes of money above mentioned to be paid by the said James Pennyman Esq. have been **by** the said James Pennyman Esq. and his assigns really paid since his composition at Goldsmiths Hall.

(Signed) JAMES PENNYMAN.

Jurat 19 die September 1649.

John Page.

September 7, 1649.

At the Committee for Advance of Money &c.

It is ordered that Sir James Pennyman paying within fourteen days to the Trēr of this Committee the some of fifty pounds that then he be respited till the middle of the next term to be heard touching the estate he hath in reversion after his father.

ED. HOWARD.
THO. JERVOISE.
HEN. MARDEN.
JOH. DOVE.
J. HUTCHINSON.

Received the first of October 1649 of Sir James Pennyman fifty pounds according to the order above written.

WILL. LANE. Trēr.

AFFIDAVIT OF SIR JAMES PENNYMAN.

Sir James Pennyman of Ormesbie in the county of Yorke knight maketh oath that James Pennyman of Ormesbie aforesaid his father payeth and is to pay £100 per an. to the Vicar of Maske and Gisborough for ever. He also maketh oath that the said James Pennyman (his father) payeth and is to pay to Thomas Ruddock during his life £20 per an. He likewise maketh oath that the said James Pennyman (his father) payith and is to pay to Mrs. Kingsley & her heires for ever £50 per an.

JAMES PENNYMAN.

Jur. 1 die October 1649.

John Page.

No. 521. SIR WILLIAM PENNYMAN, BART.

G 11. p. 109.   29 Aug. 1650.

On petition of Sir Gervase Elwes & Jeremy Elwes esqr. desiring to compound for the Manors of Egton & Skelton & the "allome mines" in Skelton sequestered for the delinquency of Sir William Pennyman Bart. with abatement of such debts as the said premises are subject to. Referred to Mr. Brereton.

G 79. p. 625.

Petition of Lord Darcy & Conyers that being heir at law to the Lady Ann Pennyman, deceased, whereby certain lands descend to him sequestered for her delinquency, & on the petition of Sir Gervase Elwes knt. & Jeremy Elwes both deceased the Committee ordered that they should enjoy the lands till their monies & arrears should be satisfied, & that afterwards the lands should come to the use of the Parliament now as they have enjoyed the lands ever since & received the profits they must be fully satisfied. Your petitioner prays that Gervas & Jeremy heirs to Sir Gervas & Jeremy account for what they have received & that he may be admitted to compound for the estate as a discoverer thereof and have it discharged.

G 79. p. 623.   15 Feb. 1653-54.

Wm. Toomer, assignee of Lord Darcy, puts in information of the discovery of the estate.

G 25. p. 295.   15 Feb. 1653-4.

It having been discovered to us by Wm. Toomer that lands sequestered for the delinquency of Sir William Pennyman & Dame Ann his wife were allowed to Sir Jervas and Jeremy Elwes, Ordered that they show cause to us by Tuesday why the premises should not be re-sequestered, & that they put in their account as to what they have received, for it is stated they have received more than their debts.

G 25. p. 300.   21 Feb. 1653-4.

Three weeks time to be given to Mr. Jeremy Elwes to appear & Mrs. Elwes his mother has undertaken to send for him.

G 25. p. 300.   22 Feb. 1653-4.

Security of £2000 to be given for the repayment of what money shall appear to have been received more than the debt.

G 25. p. 312.   14 March 1653-4.

Mr. Brereton to report the state of the whole case, & all parties to attend him.

No. 359. William Pennyman, of Gray's Inn, Gent.

G 219. p. 23.

Report. His delinquency that he was in the late wars; he saith he was never sequestered, but is now discovered by the Lady Moore, therefore you ordered him to be sequestered. He is possessed of a gelding, some wearing apparel, & books to the value of 100 marks.

23 April, 1650.   Jo. Readinge.

Fine at a sixth £11 2 3.

5 May 1650. (G 8. p. 26).

G 219. p. 28. *Petition.* (As in the Report).

G 219. p. 26. *Particular of Estate.* (As in the Report).

G 8. p. 63.   21 May, 1650.
   Discharged.

No. 537. John Metcalfe of Taunton.

G 143. p. 413.   15 March 1653-4.

Petition of Ralfe Rimer, William Penniman, Roger Talbott, & Richard Trotter. That John Metcalfe late of Taunton, parish of Stokesley, did by his last will devise unto your petitioners certain lands in Taunton in trust for payment of debts & children's portions & the maintenance of his wife. That the lands are under sequestration for the recusancy only of the said John Metcalfe who is dead. They pray the discharge of the sequestration that they may perform their trusts.

G 23. p. 1638.

Claim allowed and sequestration discharged with arrears from the date of the petition.

APPENDIX K.

EXTRACTS FROM THE NORTH RIDING RECORDS.

These records contain several interesting Pennyman entries. For a considerable period there are lists of the justices attending Quarter Sessions. These Sessions were during a period extending from 1624 to 1718 held at various places, at distances varying from seven to fifty miles from Ormesby, which latter was no small journey to undertake in those days. We find them held most often at " Thirske " (Thirsk), also at " Stoxley " (Stokesley), " Hemsley " or " Helmesley " (Helmsley), Northallerton (sometimes " North Allerton "), " New Malton " (Malton), " Beedall " (Bedale), Richmond, " Yarome " (Yarm), and Guisbrough.

During this period Sir William Pennyman, the builder of Marske Hall and famous Royalist soldier, who was High Sheriff in April 1636, attended eleven times; Sir James Pennyman 42 times (1635—1676); Sir Thomas Pennyman, High Sheriff in the 1702—1703, no less than 63 times, beginning in 1671 and making his last attendance in 1707; and Mr. William Pennyman 49 times (1689—1716).

The following entries are interesting:

Apud Yarome. 21 Sep. 1624.

> It is offered by Sir David Foulis, Knt. and Baronett, and William Penniman, Esq., two of his M[ties] Justices of peace within ye N. R. of ye Countie of Y., on ye behalfe of ye sd. N.R., yt att a generall Qr. Sessions to be holden within ye sd. N.R. there shalbe an order made for ye securinge of cc[h] ordered by ye Judges of Assizes to be paid by ye Inhab[ts] of the C. of D. towardes ye repaire of Yarome Br., yf upon triall by lawe it shall appeare yt ye said C. of D. is not liable to beare ye charge thereof as well as ye sd. Countie of Yorke. (Vol. III., p. 53.)

Helmesley. 1637.

Recites a bond entered into by Henrie Belassise, Esquier, Sir John Hotham, Knt. and Barr., Sir William Penyman, Barr., Sir Hugh Cholmeley, Knt., Thomas Heblethwaite and Rog. Wyrell, Esquires: according to the tennor and effect of one rule made in his Maties Court of King's Bench, in a cause there depending to be tried betweene .... and the Inhabts. of Bishoppricke of Duresme and the inhabs. of ye N. R. concerninge ye repaireing of Yarome Br. (Page 57.)

In the records of the same Sessions, Sir W. Pennyman appears as William Peniman de Marske, baronett, Sir William Penniman, and Sir William Penniman, baronett. We also read in the bond of several "Justic' ad pacem infra dictum Ep'atum Dunelm," and of "Yarome bridge super rivum de Tease."

Thirske. Ap. 27, 1625.

Rob. Hodgson, of Saltburn, labr., fined 3s. 6d. for stealing an ewe at Marske, from William Penniman, Esq. (Vol. III., p. 231.)

Northallerton. 19 April, 1626.

Certificate given by Sir David Foulis and William Penniman, Esq., to the effect that Margt. wife of Tho. Midleton, senr., of Midleton-on-Leaven, gent. had taken the Oath of Allegiance ....and had attended at the chapel of Midleton ....; like certificates .... from the said Justices touching .... Luke Anderson, of Tollesby, the latter never having been and not being now a Popish Recusant, as certified by the Vicar of Marton, and others. (Vol. III., p. 259.)

Helmesley. 10th Janry., 1631-2.

The pannell present..................the inhabts. of Stokesley for not repairing the highway near the Leaven, leadinge the Kinges Maties leige people from the Parsonage of Stokesley .... unto a bridge called Penniman bridge over the said Leaven into the towne and market of Stokesley. (Vol. III., p. 325.)

Thirske. 8 April, 1635.

Before Jas. Penniman and others. An agreement made by the Justices within the N. R. for devideing themselves into the severall Wapentacks and Libertyes......... Sir Will. Pennyman, Bart.......... Jas. Pennyman, Esqre., in Langbargh. (Vol. IV., p. 29.)

Thirske. Oct., 1661.

Sir Jas. Pennyman hath paid unto the Warden of Yarm Bridge ...... £50 ...... towards repair. (Vol. VI., p. 44.)

Stoxley. July, 1685.

Sir Thos. Pennyman certifies that a man has now but one chimney, the other being readie to fall to the ground, he hath utterlie taken away as being all together uselesse to him: therefore he humbly desires that he may be exempted from paying the duty of hearth money for any more than one. (Vol. VIII., p. 80.)

At Helmsley. Jan. 14, 1717-8.

An Order to be made for the Parish Officers of Ormsby to build a cottage or cottages upon the waiste for the poor people, by the consent of Sir Jas. Pennyman, Lord of the Mannor;..................... whereas Sir Jas. Pennyman, Lord of the Mannor of Ormsby, and Ralph Elgy, Overseers of the poor, and Rob. Jackson, Churchwarden of the said parish and Constablery, by their indenture bearing date the 30th day of this instant January, by them legally executed and allowed in open Court, have agreed that thirty-five yards in length and six yards in breadth of land of the waistes or commons of the said mannor, in the town street of Ormsby, near the bottom of the said town street, betwixt the houses of Nich. Pearson and Tho. Kempby, in the most convenient place, should be allotted for the building of four cottages or convenient dwelling houses for impotent poor people, now destitute of habitation, at the general charge of the parish of Ormsby aforesaid, to be taxed and gathered according to 43 Elizth.: it is, by the majority of the Justices at the Sessions aforesaid assembled, Ordered that the said cottages be erected or sett upon the said parcell of ground according to the said agreement. (Vol. VIII., p. 160.)

[North Riding Records, Vols. I. to IX., and New Series, Vols. I. to III. searched.]

G
9
P

APPENDIX L.

PENNYMAN MONUMENTAL INSCRIPTIONS.

(N.B.—There are a quantity of Arms on Monuments in Ormesby and Stainton churches, and at Christchurch, Oxford; also probably in Beverley Minster.)

1. ORMESBY CHURCH.

Sacred
To the Memory of
Sir William Henry Pennyman,
Baronet,
Who died at Ormesby Hall,
On the 9th of May, 1852,
In his 89th year.
His remains are interred,
Together with those of Charlotte,
His beloved wife,
In the Minster at Beverly,
In the East Riding of this County.
This tablet
Is intended to record
The deeply grateful affection
Which his excellent virtues,
Amiable qualities,
And extensive benevolence,
Called forth
In those who knew him most
A memorial
Of the profound respect
And veneration
In which his life was held,
And with which his name
Will ever be honoured.

Here lieth the body of
JAMES PENNYMAN, of Ormsby, Esqr.,
Eldest son of SR. JAMES PENNYMAN,
of Thornton, Bart., who died the 15th Day
of December, 1743, Aged 50 Years.
He married DOROTHY, one of ye Daughters
and Co-heiresses of DR. WILLIAM WAKE,
late Lord Archbishop of Canterbury,
Who by her Will directed this Monument,
In Memory of her beloved Husband.
She died in London, on the 2d Day of Decr.,
1754, Aged 55 Years,
And is buried in the Church at Croydon,
in ye County of Surrey, near ye Remains
of her Father and Mother.

---

2. BEVERLEY MINSTER.

NEAR this place, lie interred the remains of
Ralph Pennyman, Esqr.,
Youngest son of Sir James Pennyman, Baronet,
of Ormesby, in Cleveland: he died
August 10th, 1768, Aged 66 Years.
AND of Bridget Pennyman, his Widow,
Daughter of William Gee, Esqr., of Bishop Burton,
in the County of York.
She died, June 7th, 1774, Aged 73 Years.
THIS MEMORIAL
is erected, as a Tribute of filial affection, by their
Daughters Charlotte Bethell, Widow of William
Bethell, Esqr., of Rise, in the County of York;
and Dorothy Worsley, Widow of the Revd. James
Worsley, of Hovingham, in the County of York.

(*North.*) Sacred
To the Memory of
Sir William Henry Pennyman, Baronet,
of Ormesby Hall in Cleveland,
Who died on the 9th of May, 1852,
Aged 88 years.
The Seventh Baronet of the Name
Which he lived to adorn,
By his many and unceasing virtues,
Afectionate and Benevolent.
In his private Relations,
His Bearing
was Gentle and Benign to all,
Honoured and Reverenced
In his Life-time,
In Death he leaves behind a Name
To be Remembered
Ever with profound Respect,
And affectionate Keeping.
This Monument is erected
By his only surviving
And affectionate sister,
F. H. Robinson.

(*North.*) Sacred
To the Memory
of
Charlotte,
The beloved Wife of
Sir William Pennyman, Baronet,
Of Ormesby Hall in
Cleveland;
Who departed this life at Beverley,
On the 3rd day of May, 1848,
Aged 82 years.
"I heard a voice from Heaven saying
Unto me, Write, Blessed are the dead
Which die in the Lord from hence-
forth: Yea, saith the Spirit, That
They may rest from their labours,
And their works may follow them."

(*North.*)

To the Memory of
Dorothy,
The widow of
The Revnd. James Worseley,
Rector of Stonegrave,
in the
North Riding of the County of York,
and the youngest Daughter of
Ralph Pennyman, Esqre.,
of This Town,
descended from the family of
Pennyman,
of Ormesby in Cleveland.
She died the 14th of November, 1811,
in the 72nd year of her age,
and lies here interred.

This Monument is erected,
as a Token of filial
Affection,
by her surviving daughter
Dorothy,
The wife of the Revd. Nicholas Holme,
of Rise.

(*Left of East Window.*)

Sacred to the Memory of
Warton Pennyman Berry, Esq., Grandson of Sir Warton Pennyman Warton, Bart., who died 8th of Feb., 1840, in the 18th year of his age. He was Captain in the Old East Yorks. Militia, & for many years a resident of this town, and his remains are deposited in a vault below, adjoining those of his sister, Mary Pennyman Ellison.

(*Left of East Window.*)

To the Memory of
Thomas Pennyman, Esq.,
Third son of Sir James Pennyman, of Thornton in Cleveland, in the County of Yorks., Bart., by Dame Mary his wife, dau. of Michael Warton, Esq., of Beverley Parks, in the County of York, East Riding, by Sousanna Paulet, dau. of Lord Paulet, of Hinton St. George in Somerset, Who departed this life, 30th of July, in the Year of our Lord, 1759, aged 60 Y., 3 M., 14 D.

(*Right of East Window.*)

Sir Warton Pennyman Warton, Bart., 4th son of Sir James Pennyman, of Thornton in Cleveland, in the County of York, Bart., by Dame Mary his wife, daughter of Michael Warton, Esq., of Beverley Parks, in the County of York. He married Charlotta, 3rd dau. of Sir Charles Hotham, Bart., of Scorborough in this County, by whom he had two sons & 9 daughters, viz., James, died unmarried, Major of the Queen's Regt. of Dragoons; Charles, died an Infant; Charlotta, married to Francis Boynton, Esq., 2nd son of Sir Francis Boynton, bart., of Agnes Burton in the County of York; Mary, married to Mr. William Berry, ... Philippa and Dorothy died unmarried; Margaret, mar. Henry Maister, Esq., of Winestead, Yorks.; Harriot, married Henry Stapylton, Esq., of Wighill Park, Yorks.; Caroline, mar. Robert Gee, Esq. of Bishop Burton in Yorks.; Diana, mar. Geo. Hotham, Esq., 5th son of Sir Beaumont Hotham, Bart., of Scorbrough, Yorks. He died on 14th Jan., 1770, aged 69 years, 7 months, & 14 days. His surviving daughters have caused this monument to be erected to his memory.

(*South.*)

In the Vault beneath,
Are intered the Remains of
Mary, the Widow of
William Berry, Esqre.,
And second daughter of
Sir Warton Pennyman
Warton, Bart.
She died on the 19th of April, 1789,
Aged 60 years.
Also the Remains of
Mary Pennyman, only surviving
Daughter of the above
William and Mary Berry,
And wife of
Henry Elison, Esqre.,
of this Place,
Born June 4th, 1758,
Died September 25th, 1826.

Sacred
To the Memory of the above,
This Monument was erected
by William Elison, Esqre.,
In the year 1834.

3. STAINTON CHURCH.*

(*Tablet near Altar Steps.*)

To the Memory of
Dame Mary Pennyman,
Wife of Sir James Pennyman, Bar.,
Daughter of
Michael Warton of Beverley, Esqr.,
by Susanna his wife,
who was Daughter of
John, Lord Pawlett, of Hinton
St. George, in Somersetshire.
This worthy Lady Departed this life
Novr. 9th, 1727, Aged 65.

---

* Stainton, about 4½ miles West of Ormesby. It is the parish in which Thornton, where so many Pennymans lived, is a hamlet. In fact, the old Pennyman house at Thornton was only about 300 yards from Stainton Church.

MONUMENTAL INSCRIPTIONS. 107

(Tablet on North Side, over Choir Stalls.)

To the Memory of
Miss Maria Pennyman,
who Departed this life
the 11th April, 1714,
Aged 16.
She was Daughter of
Sir James Pennyman, Bart.,
by Dame Mary, his wife.

(Tablet on South Side, over Choir Stalls.)

Near to this place
are deposited the remains of
Sir James Pennyman, Baronet,
Who departed this life the
27th day of March, 1808,
Aged 72 years.

(Tablet on South Side, near Chancel Steps.)

To the Memory of
Sir James Pennyman, Bart.,
who departed this life
The 17th Decr., 1745, Aged 82.

(Tablet on South Side, over Chancel Door.)

Hic jacet
Gulielmus Pennyman, Baronettus.
Obiit xvi^{to} Apr. MDCCLXVIII,
Ætatis suæ LXXII.

(Small Tablet over Vestry Door.)

Sacred to the memory of
Hannah Pennyman,
Who departed this life,
The 10th day of June, 1836, aged 63 years.
She was the second daughter of
Sir James Pennyman, Bart.,
and Elizabeth, his wife,
Who was daughter of
Sir Henry Grey,
of Howick, in the County
of Northumberland, baronet.

4. LITTLE PONTON, near Grantham, co. Lincoln.

To the Memory
of William Pennyman, Esqr.,
Who died July the 12th, 1806,
Aged 52 years.
Also John Henry Pennyman, Esqr.,
Major in the Cinque Port Light Dragoons,
Who died Nov. the 15th, 1795,
Aged 40 years.
Two dutiful & affectionate sons
of James Pennyman, Esq., of Little Paunton,
and Dorothy his wife.
This tablet is inscribed as a Tribute of Affection,
by their surviving Parent, and truly afflicted Mother.

In Memory of
Henry Pennyman, Esq.,
Son of Sr Thomas Pennyman, Bart., of
Ormsby in Cleveland, Yorkshire,
Who dyed August 21, 1754,
Aged 74.
And of Elizabeth, his wife,
Sister of
William Daye, Esq.,
who dyed March 22d., 1749,
Aged 68.

In Memory of
William Daye, Esqre.,
who died the 8th of April, 1741, In the
66th year of his age.

(*Arms.*—Per chevron argent and azure, 3 mullets counterchanged.)

5. CHRIST CHURCH CATHEDRAL, Oxford.

M. S.
H. S. E. Guil. Pennyman Baronettus
equestri dignitate parique fortuna
decorus
obsequio et fide adversus optimum eundemqe afflictissimum
Principum Carolum R. spectabilis
qui
ineunte nuper execranda rebellione statim in partes transgressus
Sereniss: Regem
(cum cœtera inermis classe, armamentariis, arcibus, omnibusq belli
prœsidiis orbatus, nudo majestatis titulo armatus staret)
duobus cohortibus, equitum una, peditum altera
a se conscriptis primum instruxit
quibus et ipse præfuit tribunus; ac brevi urbis Oxon
præfectura donatus est in qua ita se gessit
ut nec decessor Ashlæus nec successor Ashtonus (magna bello nom'na)
luminibus ipsius obstruerunt
Demum
febre epidemica correptus in medio ætatis honorumqe decursu
præmature extinctus triste sui desiderium apud omnes reliquit
quibus morum suavitate ac comitate fuerat merito charissimus
Obiit XXII August A.D. MDCXLIII.
Tumulo potitus in eadem domo in qua
primum ingenii cultum capessiverat.
B. M. T. P. S.
Anna conjux charissima quæ cum hæreditate luculenta
familae alias honestae
Bironae et Conieriae familiar: lucem intulit
Vixit una conjunctissime sine ulla offensa
Mortuo demum marito
Quasi tristis divorcii moras pertæsa
morbo opportuna indulgens alacris ac intrepida
vitæ nuncium remisit ut vel sic
redderetur marito
Obiit XII Julii. A.D. MDCLIV.
illata est tumulo dulcissimi mariti
Jul. XVIII.

As some of the readers of this may not be Latin scholars, the following may be given as a rough translation :—

> Here lies buried Sir William Pennyman, Bart.,
> With knightly rank and knightly fortune ennobled
> For duty and loyalty to the best and at the same time most
> unfortunate of princes, King Charles, conspicuous,
> Who lately
> At the beginning of the detestable rebellion marched at once
> to the standard of his most serene majesty
> (When defenceless, shorn of fleets, troops, strongholds, and
> all the muniments of war, he stood armed with
> the bare name of Majesty)
> And furnished him first with two regiments, one of foot and
> one of horse, raised by himself,
> Which he commanded himself: and shortly had conferred on him
> the command of the City of Oxford: in which he so bore himself,
> That neither his predecessor Ashley nor his successor Ashton
> (two great names in the war) eclipsed his fame.
> At length
> Seized with an epidemic fever, in mid course of life and honours
> He was prematurely cut off, leaving all to mourn and miss him,
> to whom he had been deservedly beloved for his genial and
> courteous manners.
> He died August 22nd, 1643.
> Anna, his beloved wife, brought him the honour of a noble
> ancestry, born of the families of Biron and Conyers.
> She lived a most united life without offence
> And at length when her husband was dead
> As if wearied with long days of drear divorce
> Accepted a welcome death and straightway fearlessly
> Obtained separation from life that even so
> She might be restored to her husband.
> She died July 12th, 1654,
> And was placed in the grave of her beloved husband on July 18th.

Arms Pennyman.—Impaling a quarterly shield.

6. ALL SAINTS' CHURCH, North Street, York.

At the east end of the North Aisle in this Church, there is a stone with three inscriptions on it. The first is in memory of Johane, wife of Joh. Stoddart, Rector of the Church, who was buried in 1599. Half-way down the stone is :—

> Here lieth ye Body of Mr. James
> Pennyman (son of Thos. Pennyman)
> Dr. of Divinity, who Departed this
> Life ye 7th of Feb., 168$\frac{8}{9}$, & in ye 43 year
> of his age.
> As allso Mrs. Esther Pennyman
> his Wife, who Dyed ye 10th of
> August 1745, Aged 87.
> (The above Dr. Pennyman was Rector of Stokesley. See p. 16)

Then in a corner at the bottom of the stone comes—

> John Stoddart Clerke,
> Parson of this
> Rectory induct
> here, vj Marche 1593.

There is also a stone in the South Aisle with the name of Pennyman on it, but the rest of the inscription has been worn away by the tread of countless feet.

G
9

G
9

APPENDIX M.

MS. PENNYMAN NOTICES.

No. 3. BODLEIAN LIBRARY MSS.

MS. Browne Willis 71, *fo.* 18. Epitaph of William Pennyman, bart., 1643.

MS. Tanner 67, *p.* 59. Acquittance given by Sir Wm. Pennyman to Archbishop Laud for £250, Dec. 22, 1639.

MS. Rawl. A 241, *fo.* 259b. Appointment of Thomas Pennyman to be receiver general of the duties upon vellum etc. 30 Sept. 1698.

MS. Rawl. C 254, *fo.* 27. Notice from the epitaph of Sir Wm. Pennyman, governor of Oxford, 1643.

MS. Rawl. D 1092, *fo.* 204. Letter from Chas. Pennyman, Univ. Coll., Oxford, with account of a quarrel with Robt. Knapp, 1704.

MS. Rawl. D 923, *fos.* 279b.—280. Notice of Wm. Pennyman, one of the clerks in chancery, and his son William.

MS. Rawl. D 682, *fo.* 18. Epitaphs on Sir Wm. Pennyman and his wife in Christ Church, Oxford, 1643-4.

No. 4. HAILSTONE MSS. IN YORK MINSTER LIBRARY.

1629-1714. Schedule of several Settlements and deeds relating to the Manor of Welburn. (Pennymans parties to several of them.)
    Box 3. 19.

1650. June 24. Wm. Pennyman of Gray's Inn gent. to Sir John Gibson of Welburn kt., and John Gibson, esqr., his son and heir apparent. Deed of Defeazance for redeeming Sunley Hill in Welburne, parish of Kirkdale, within 7 years.
    Box 3. 6.

1657. May 14. Wm. Pennyman to Geo. Grainge and John Pearson. Bargain & Sale of Sunley Hill in Welburn.
    Box 3. 6.

1657. June 9. Geo. Grainge of Eston co. York, gent., and John Pearson of Ormsby, yeoman, to John Gibson of Welburn esqr., and Wm. Pennyman of Durham, esqr. Declaration of Trust as to Sunley Hill.

Box 3. 6.

1740. June 7. Matt. Thompson, of Middleham, 1st pt., Richd. Beck of Melmerby yeoman, 2nd pt., Sir James Pennyman of Thornton, bart., 3rd pt., and Warton Warton of Beverley esqr., 4th pt. Memorial of deed.

pp 61.

MARRIAGE LICENCES AND ALLEGATIONS
in the Faculty Office of the Archbishop of Canterbury, 1521-1869.

1692. Oct. 24. James Pennyman of Ormesby co. York esquire, bachelor, æt. 25, and Mary Wharton* of St. Anne's Westminster spinster, æt. 24. Her parents are dead. To be married at St. Margaret's Westminster, on .... (blank).

MARRIAGE LICENCES AND ALLEGATIONS
in the Registry of the Bishop of London.

1703. June 17. Thomas Pennyman of Lincoln's Inn, bachelor, aged 34, and Margt. Angier of Nothaw. co. Hertford spr. aged 21. At St. Martin in the Fields.

1594. Dec. 18. Wm. Pennyman of the Inner Temple London gent. and Anne Tottle of Harmondsworth co. Midx. spr. dau. of Rd. T. late of St. Dunstan in the West decd. General licence (that is, to be married at any church in the diocese).

MARRIAGE LICENCES AND ALLEGATIONS
in the Faculty Office of the Bishop of London.

1681. Aug. 1. Wm. Pennyman of the Middle Temple London esqr. baehr. about 24, and Annabella Browne spr. about 18, dau. of Sir Rd. B. knt. and bart. of Debdon co. Essex, who consents. (At St. Andrew's Holborn, or Lincoln's Inn Chapel.)

*Her name was Warton. J.W.P.

28 July 1933

Dr Josiah Penlman,
Provost, University of Pennsylvania.

My dear Provost,

I understand that you are interested in the Pennyman (Penniman, Penniman family — the name is variantly written in old records) and that you claim-descent from James Pennyman who came on the 'Lyon' to Boston, Massachusetts,1631. No accurate and authentic record of the parentage of this James Pennyman was known until I recently discovered it after considerable search. The Pennymans of Ormesby in this County knew nothing of this James, and his name is omitted in the account of the family written by one of them. (By the way the present Pennymans of Ormesby took by Royal Licence that name in 1853,been previously known by their family name of Worsley). When in London during the Spring and part of this Summer I went thoroughly into the matter; I examined the manuscript pedigrees in the British Museum Library, the Pennyman references at the Record Office,Chancery Lane, and Penniman wills at Somerset House. Since I returned to Yorkshire I have examined the Pennyman wills at York Registry,and from the material I have collected I have been able to draw up the first complete and authentic Pedigree of the family of Pennyman of Yorkshire, Lincolnshire, Lancashire,and county Middlesex. I have seen certain American books which contain reference

APPENDIX N.

AMERICAN PENNIMANS.

Note on the Genealogy of the American families of Penniman.

In the year 1898 Mr. Pennyman had some correspondence with the Rev. George Wallace Penniman, of Massachussets, who was collecting material for a work on the Penniman family in America; he found that some American Pennimans believed their ancestors to have been Pennymans of Ormesby; and that all of the American Pennimans appear to descend from James Penniman, supposed by some to have been a younger brother of Sir William Pennyman, the distinguished Royalist soldier, who was Governor of Oxford for King Charles; that this same James Pennyman married Lydia, daughter of Benet Eliot of Nazing in Essex, and that they emigrated to New England, sailing, with the brothers John and Jacob Eliot, on the ship "Lion," which landed on Nov. 2nd 1631.

Now Mr. Pennyman's family records not only show no trace of the supposed emigrant, but give a certain amount of negative evidence against his existence, at any rate in this particular place in the pedigree. Firstly there is Dugdale's visitation. In 1665 Sir William Dugdale, Norroy King of Arms, came to York and summoned the heads of the chief county families to come in and prove their pedigrees. Sir James Pennyman of Ormesby proved his; he gave in its proper place the name of Sir W. Pennyman of Marske, the Governor of Oxford, but made no mention of any brother of his. Now as Sir James Pennyman was aged 58 at the date of the visitation, and was first cousin to Sir W. Pennyman, he must have known of the emigration of another first cousin in 1631, 34 years previously. Secondly, the father of the supposed emigrant, in his will makes no mention of any younger son, and leaves property to his eldest son William, and in default of him and his issue, over to nephews, nieces, and his brother at Ormesby, but not to a younger son (see app. C., p. 25.) An ingenious surmise has been made which much lessens the force of this negative evidence. An emigrant at that date would be a Puritan; and the strong Royalist Pennyman family may very likely have thought

APPI

AMERICA

Note on the Genealogy o

In the year 1898 Mr. Pen
Rev. George Wallace Penni
material for a work on the I
some American Penniman
mans of Ormesby; and tha
descend from James Pen
younger brother of Sir W
soldier, who was Governor
James Pennyman married
Essex, and that they er
brothers John and Jaco
on Nov. 2nd 1631.
Now Mr. Pennyman's
supposed emigrant, but
against his existence, at
Firstly there is Dugd
Norroy King of Arms,
chief county families t
Pennyman of Ormesby
of Sir W. Pennyman
mention of any broth
58 at the date of the
he must have known
years previously. S
will makes no men
—eldest son William,
nieces, and his bro
p.25.) An ingenio
of this negative ev
and the strong Ro

private and personal.

Howden,
Yorkshire.
England.
28 July 1933

Dr Josiah Peniman,
Provost, University of Pennsylvania.

My dear Provost,

I understand that you are interested in the Pennyman (Penniman, Pealman family —— the name is variantly written in old Records) and that you claim descent from James Pennyman who came on the 'Lyon' to Boston, Massachusetts,1631. No accurate and authentic record of the parentage of this James Pennyman was known until I recently discovered it after considerable search. The Pennymans of Ormesby in this County knew nothing of this James, and his name is omitted in the account of the family written by one of them. (By the way the present Pennymans of Ormesby took by Royal Licence that name in 1853, been previously known by their family name of Worsley). When in London during the Spring and part of this Summer I went thoroughly into the matter; I examined the manuscript pedigrees in the British Museum Library, the Pennyman references at the Record Office, Chancery Lane, and Penniman wills at Somerset House. Since I returned to Yorkshire I have examined the Pennyman wills at York Registry, and from the material I have collected I have been able to draw up the first complete and authentic Pedigree of the family of Pennyman of Yorkshire, Lincolnshire, Lancashire, and county Middlesex. I have seen certain American books which contain reference to the Pennimans of America, (how they trace back to Sir William Penniman of Ormesby, a Royalist, whose "Crest" "may still be seen upon the walls of Christ Church, Oxford".) I wonder how the American Pennimans can trace descent from a gentleman who died without issue. Or was Sir William Penniman of Ormesby : he lived at Marske : quite a different place). There is an inscription to his memory in Christ Church, Oxford, and that is about the only thing that is correct in that account. This Sir William Pennyman, who was created a Baronet, 6 May 1628, was son of William Pennyman, whose will is dated 1628, and grandson of James Pennyman of Ormesby by his first wife. But he has nothing whatever to do with James Pennyman, the American settler of 1631. It is better to have authentic facts, particularly as regards Family History, and this often takes much search. I can assure you that as a descendant of James Pennyman, the Puritan, you have a fine ancestry, and that you do spring from the Ormesby family, but at a date earlier than the Sir William Pennyman quoted in the American book.

I copied the original pedigrees, including the one drawn up by William Segar, Norroy King of Arms, with drawing of the Arms and Crest, which I also copied, and I will send you the whole pedigree with the Arms, etc, if you care to send me $10, to go towards my personal expenses in obtaining the data. I really ought to ask a great deal more, but I will state $10, and if you care to send more it will be acceptable. Please send in American Dollars bills which I can cash easily here. I am a professional genealogist, and have recntly done work for Lord Howard de Walden, the Duchess of Norfolk, and several other prominent families. I go a lot of emblazon the Pennyman arms on parchment for $50. I go a lot of heraldic painting for English clients. Compliments,

Yours very truly,
F.H.Sunderland.

from: F.H.Sunderland.

a Puritan relative such a disgrace, as to be only too glad to seize his emigration as an opportunity to disinherit and disavow him.

Still, even if the negative evidence can be discounted, positive evidence of his identity and place in the family tree is wanting. There is one slight corroboration of the story, viz., the undoubted existence of Pennimans at Braintree, Mass., the point of which is that there is a Braintree in Essex, not very far from Nazing.

Another descent of the American Pennimans has been given Mr. Pennyman:—

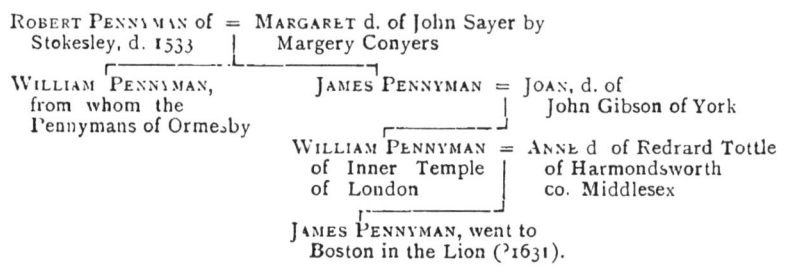

```
ROBERT PENNYMAN of    =  MARGARET d. of John Sayer by
  Stokesley, d. 1533   |   Margery Conyers
  ┌───────────────────┴────────────────┐
WILLIAM PENNYMAN,           JAMES PENNYMAN  =  JOAN, d. of
  from whom the                             |   John Gibson of York
  Pennymans of Ormesby      ┌───────────────┘
                           WILLIAM PENNYMAN  =  ANNE d of Redrard Tottle
                             of Inner Temple |    of Harmondsworth
                             of London       |    co. Middlesex
                            ┌────────────────┘
                           JAMES PENNYMAN, went to
                             Boston in the Lion ('1631).
```

Mr. Pennyman has evidence that a licence was granted on 18 Dec. 1594 for a marriage between William Pennyman of the Inner Temple and Anne d. of Rd. Tottle. Otherwise he knows nothing of this pedigree or whether there is any evidence to support it.

It will be a cause of much satisfaction to Pennymans and Pennimans alike if evidence can be found to establish the relationship.

1

APPENDIX O.

MISCELLANEOUS.

1. 1662, Sept. 30. [Hailstone MSS., Box 319.]

Letter from SIR JOHN GIBSON, of Welburne, knt.

Sonne,
Dat pira dat poma qui non habet alia dona. I can but (like the Beggar) returne you thankes for your great care and paines you have taken in the Earle of Straffordes businesse, thoughe the Result did not answere your desires. The sick and sad distemper of my cosen Dr. Pennyman's wife hath caused my daughters absence at present from home, who is now at Stoxley. Wee are all in good health (God be thanked) hoping you are soe too after your iowrney. All is well at Welburne, your harvest well got in, your seed well sowne, and cominge up againe, covering the browne fallow wth. a greene Carpet, your Coachhouse is well theaked, only your Well comes but drylie off this drought, your Appleharvest is almost compleated, if the last flood hed not recruited your pondes your pikes had suffered for want of water. Young George Spanton like the Spring renews his strenght, but Mr. Taylor like the time of the yeare, is an Autumne condition. My cosen Anne Bradshaw presents her respects to you. There is a warrant come from the head Constable to send in a horse this afternoone at two of the clocke to Helmsley well mounted, wth. a weeks pay, compleatly arm'd wth. powder and ball, what the meaning of it should be I know not, except it be to guard the Duke of Buckingham, who they say is coming to live at York. I have writt a letter to Captaine Tankerd to desire him to excuse your horse for not appearing, you being absent, and at your returne (if need require) he shall have one sent in. My blessing remembred to you, wishing you well home, I take leave and remaine Your loving father,

JOHN GIBSON.

September the last
this Tuesday morning
 1662.

Addressed:—"ffor his very loving sonne John Gibson esqr. at York."

Note—The writer of this letter was Sir John Gibson, of Welburne, son of Sir John Gibson, of Welburne, knt., and grandson of Sir John Gibson, knt., and Vicar-General to the Archbishop of York. In 1650 the writer was a prisoner in Durham Gaol for non-payment of a Bond given as surety for John Redmayne, of Fulford, esq., whose son Robert Redmayne repudiated the debt in 1662. There is a good deal of very curious correspondence about the matter in the same bundle of the Hailstone MSS. The John Gibson to whom the letter was written, married Joane, daughter of James Pennyman, of Ormesby, esq. (See his will in appendix C., No. 7.) Sir John Gibson, the father, died in June 1665

2. 1698, July 16.

Letter from JOHN SAUNDERS to his son-in-law James Pennyman, esq.*

" To James Pennyman, esq., at his house at Hutton Lockris, near Gisborow in Cleveland, present this with care and speed."

York, July the 16th '98.
Son,

I think this will come to your hands soon after your coming from the Spaw, and I thought good to let you know something concerning Houses at York, that which your wife saw they Aske Twelve Pounds a yeare for without Coach House and Stable. I doubt that House is to far from the Church for you. Here is another Brick House in Tanners Row on the Back side of Michall Gate that is larger then the other and hath better Roomes, and very good Clossetts, and a very pretty Garden Planted and Walled about with Brick and a very good Sommer House in it and extraordinary good Sellering, it is not above a Stones Throw from three good Churches that is All Saints', St. Johns, and our St. Martins, but there is no Stable to this House but you may have one very nere hand. This latter House belongs to one Mr. Rowland Playse. I cannot tell whether you know him. I think my Bro. Trotter does, his Brother that lives here at the Mannor is imployed to lett it, he Askes Ten Pounds a yeare for it and I think it worth it. If you like a private retired place you can-not I think be better fitted, you may Ride or Walk out of Michall Gate or the Postern without being seen by them in the High Street. If you will come to live at York before Winter it may be that each of these Houses may be taken somewhat cheeper. And wee thinke it your wiseist course so to Doe, and to take your time to put off Cattle, Corne and Hay and Winter Eateage and for ordering of Servants; If you should keep Goods to be put off at Spring, if Hay then should be scarse they would sell badly. It will be good to let what grounds you have in your hands by our Lady day next, there can be noe inconvenience

*See will of this James Pennyman, 1698, in appendix C., No. 9.

(which I can foresee) in your removeing before Winter but that you have provided your Coales, me thinks such a Towne as Gisborow should be Glad to take them off your hands before next Winter be past, many have gained by putting off Stock and ffodder before a Winter, and then it is the best time of the yeare to be in a Towne; I shall be glad to heare that you came all well Home from the Spaw, our loue and service to all ffreinds not forgetting Bro: Richard and Sis: ffalkinham, I am your loveing ffather in Law

JO: SAUNDERS.

the latter House hath an Allye on each side that goes into Michallgate Just against St. Martin's Church.

---

3.   MARGARET PENNYMAN.

From the Preface to "Miscellanies in Prose and Verse, by the Honourable Lady Margaret Pennyman. 1740."

To the Reader.

* * * * * * * *

Lady Margaret Pennyman was the only daughter of Barnet Auger, Esqr., of the City of Westminster, Carpenter to the Crown during the time of King Charles II., &c.

She was born in the year 1688, and besides her natural endowments, which were very extraordinary, she was educated in the politest Manner by having all her Tutors come home to her.

Before she was 15 years of age, she was married to Thomas Pennyman, Esqr., second son of Sir James Pennyman, Bart. (of a well-known family in Yorkshire), whose Elder Brother dying, he succeeded to the Title and Estate.

This young Lady's fortune was £2000, and the Match approved by her relations at first, tho' afterwards they would fain have broke it off, but the Amour was gone too far. Miss was honourably fixed in her resolution, which was confirmed by her putting it in execution. The Bridegroom was, at the Celebration of his Nuptials (which to be safely performed were *twice** performed) Receiver-General of the Stamp Revenue; the income of this post, and succeeding his Elder Brother, threw him into such Extravagancies as rendered this a very unhappy marriage; so that

---

* First privately at a Tavern, and afterwards *publickly* at the Parish Church of St. Martin in the Fields.

on Account of his Lewdness, and other ill-usages of his Lady, they were obliged to a separation, by Law, in less than three month's time.

Lady Pennyman having been also a fortunate Adventurer in the Mississippi-Scheme, went to Paris in 1720 to dispose of her Stock; but that year proving as fatal in France, as it was to our South-Sea-Scheme, she was therein unfortunate, and returned to England under the greatest Anxiety of Disappointment.

The following Poems and Journals of her Expedition, and the Adventures she met with, cannot fail both to *Please* and *Instruct* others, tho' it proved grievous to herself. Upon her return to England she led a most recluse Life for 13 years afterwards; died June 16, 1733, in the 46th Year of her age, and was buried by her Brother Burridge Auger, Esqr., in a vault belonging to their family, in the Church of St. Margaret, Westminster.

Note.—This story copied from the preface to a book, not now in Mr. Pennyman's possession, is impossible as it stands. The marriage seems to have taken place about 1703, and on p 116 is recorded a marriage licence between Thomas Pennyman, bachelor, aged 34, and Margt Angier, aged 21. The latter is obviously a false age. Now Sir Thomas Pennyman was in 1703 aged 61, had in 1662 married Frances Lowther and had a family, and had succeeded his father (not his elder brother) in 1679. His Son Thomas may well have been aged 34 in 1703, but he never succeeded to the title or estates. Sir Thomas' will was made in 1700, and proved in 1708. On p. 115 there is a note of the appointment of Thomas (not stated to be Sir Thomas) Pennyman to be receiver general of the duties upon vellum.

---

4. Letter from Sir James Pennyman to his sister Dorothy.

Dr. Sister,—

I was favoured with yours last post and am much hurt to find your circumstances in so bad a way. I thought that when Mr. Burton rais'd that money you would have been easy; you desire me to be bound with Mr. Worsley for a Sum of money without mentioning any Sum: now Detty you must know by your own circumstances, that whatever sum it was I should have it to pay myself, & realy I am affraid there is so much oweing that there would be no end, and no moderate Sum would avail any thing, & you must be sensible I have a large Family of my own to provide for, and I should not be doing them Justice to deprive them of much, you know I told you I would give you for your Children £1000 which I will do, and I shall pay you £40 a year the Interest towards educating them, and when they grow up to be put out to profession then it shall be devided amongst them, if really any moderate Sum would have made your circumstances easy, I should have been Happy in being the

Instrument, but as you are circumstanced I realy do not know what can be done. God Bless you and believe me your affect: Brother

JAMES PENNYMAN.

Beverley, Dec. 30th.

Endorsed:

"My Brother Sir James Pennyman Promise of one Thousand Pounds and that he will divide it equally amongst My three Boys (my Girl not being born at the time this promise was given) to put them out to professions."

---

5.   Funeral of SIR JAMES PENNYMAN, Bart.

Conducted and perform'd by Jas. Cuthbert, of Richmond, Surrey, April 6th, 1808.

	£	s.	d.
To conducting Funeral to Thornton in Yorkshire, as per contract	463	3	0
To Sundrys order'd by Mr. Hall at Stokesley, vizt:—			
Use of 6 Gentlemen's Fine Cloaks	1	4	0
6 Rich Silk Hatbands for Mourners	3	12	0
4 Pair Bearer Gloves for do.	0	10	0
2 Pair Silk Gloves for do.	0	11	6
6 Rich Silk Hatbands for Pall Bearers	3	12	0
6 Pair Bearer Gloves for do.	0	15	0
8 Silk Hatbands for Bearers	3	12	0
8 Pair Bearer Gloves for do.	1	0	0
2 Rich Armozim Scarves for Ministers	4	0	0
2 Rich Silk Hatbands for do.	1	4	0
2 Pairs Silk Gloves for do.	0	11	6
1 Rich Silk Hatband for the Clerk	0	12	0
1 Pair Bearer Gloves for do.	0	2	6
1 Rich Silk Hood for Jane Messenger	0	9	0
1 Pair Bearer Gloves for do.	0	2	6
6 Rich Silk Scarves for Pall Bearers	6	0	0
	491	1	0
Amount of Turnpik's paid	10	14	0
	£501	15	0

6. Notes of EARLY PENNYMANS, by the late Rev. Charles Best Norcliffe, but without references to the authorities.

1494. Thos. Penyman was a friar in the Carmelite house at Norwich.

1538. Was buried Nicholas Pennyman, Chaplain, and Rector of St. Martin at the Plain, in Norwich.

1565. Thos. Wrangham, clerke, parish priest of St. Andrew's, Auckland, owes to Wm. Peneman, for a bowll of haver malt lent unto him xx^d.

---

7. TANKARD OF WM. PENNYMAN, ESQ., 1578-1597.

In about the year 1894 the following announcement was sent to Mr. J. S. Pennyman :—

The following Tankard, the Property of T. Parrington, Esq., of Whitby, will be sold by Messrs. Sotheby, Wilkinson & Hodge, 13, Wellington Street, Strand, London, on Wednesday, May 20, at Three o'clock.

Peg Tankard made by J. Plummer in York, between 1578 and 1597. It stands on three ball feet, each of which is attached to the tankard by a trefoil leaf, the side is beautifully engraved with roses, lilies, sunflowers and foliage, on the lid are engraved the Pennyman Arms, surrounded by a wreath of flowers. The lid opens by two small engraved balls representing flowerbuds. The handle, which is not engraved, is deeply grooved at the back and terminates in a shield. The six pegs inside indicate six gills, the measure of the tankard. It was customary to drink to a peg, and when empty to blow the whistle in the handle. Weight 28 ozs. 2 dwts.

This celebrated tankard was made for William Pennyman, of Ormesby, Esquire, from whose descendants it passed by will to the Consett family, and thence similarly to the Dryden Family, from whom Mr. Parrington inherited it. The proprietor has in his possession the will of William Pennyman's grandson, William Pennyman, dated September 20th, 1659; in which the tankard which he calls " my flower wrought silver cann," is bequeathed to his son.

[Mr. J. W. Pennyman went to see the tankard, which was squat and ugly, and did not bid a high price. It was sold to somebody else for about £112.]

LIFE OF THOS. WENTWORTH, EARL OF STRAFFORD, by Elizth. Cooper. Vol. I. page 87.

1631. Letter to Thos. Wentworth, Earl of Stafford, from Sir W. Pennyman, who had charge of his children:—

"Now to write that news that I have, which I presume will be most acceptable. Your lordship's children are all very well, and your lordship need not fear the going forward of your building, when you have so careful a steward as Mrs. Ann. She complained to me very much of two rainy days, which, as she said, hindered her from coming down and the building from going up, because she was enforced to keep her chamber, and could not overlook the workmen."

Again:—

"At our arrival at York, we found Mr. William and Mrs. Ann, and all the rest of your lordship's family, very well. They were not a little glad to receive their tokens, and yet, they said, they would be more glad to receive your lordship and their worthy mother. We all with one vote agreed to their opinion, and wished that your lordship's occasions might be as swift and speedy in their despatch, as our thoughts and desires are in wishing them."

---

8. "PENAL LAWS AND TEST ACT," by Sir Geo. Duckett, Bart., 1882.

Questions touching their repeal propounded in 1687-8 by James II. to Deputy Lieutenants and Magistrates, through the Lord Lieutenants. (Page 93.)

Answer of Sir Thos. Pennyman Bart. of Ormesby, (Lord Privy Seal to William III.; he married Frances Lowther).

"First, If I be chosen a member of Parliament, I shall be reddy to give my vote according to the reasons of the debate in the house, and not otherwise.

Secondly, If I doe concerne myself in the election of any to serve as a member of Parliament, I shall give my vote to such, as, to ye best of my judgement, will serve the King and the Crowne faithfully and honestly.

Thirdly, I thinke myselfe obliged to live peaceably and quietly with all men, as becomes Loyall subjects."

(Signed) THOMAS PENNYMAN.

At page 104 his name appears as one of the Lieutenant Collonells in Collonell Darcy's regiment in the N. R. of Yorkshire; also that of Thos. Worsley, one of the Majors.

Thos. Worsley of Hovingham (was M.P. for Malton in 1685; he died 1715.)

His answer was:—

"1st. If I be chosen a Parliament man, I shall goe free into the house, and give my vote as my judgement and reason shall direct when I heare the debates.

2nd. If I be concerned in the election of any member, it shall be for such as I thinke will serve the King and Country faithfully and honestly.

3rd. I alwayes shall desire, and hope to live peaceably and honestly, as becomes a good Christian, and a Loyall subject.

(Signed) THOM. WORSLEY.

NOTES FROM MRS. CLOSE.

The following notes were taken down in writing by Mrs. J. S. Pennyman from Mrs. Close, a niece of the last Lady Pennyman, who spent much of her time at Ormesby during that lady's life:—

Ormesby Church was partially restored in 1810. In the family vault there are interred:—

Mr. James Pennyman, son of Sir James Pennyman, who married Miss Warton of Beverley, and died before his Father. Consequently the brother of Sir James,

Sir William Pennyman, succeeded to the title and property. He died a bachelor, and Sir Warton Pennyman succeeded him. *His* son also died young, and his large possessions, much of the Warton as well as Pennyman property, were divided among his daughters, heiresses, and scattered abroad in various families, the Hothams, Chetwynds, &c.

The Mr. James Pennyman, whose coffin is in the vault, began to build the present Hall; there had been an old one. He married the daughter of Archbishop Wake. She went on with the building, but it was finished by the last Sir James.

In 1808 Sir James Pennyman died. For thirty years previously Ormesby Hall had been completely closed. In 1809 Sir William Henry Pennyman first came there. The whole estate was then in a state of ruin; every farm and cottage falling down; the park let, in small enclosures. Sir William had five brothers who died abroad: Henry Grey, Ralph, James, Charles, and Frederick (twin brother to Mrs. Robinson), and sisters Elizabeth, Hannah, Charlotte (Mrs. Boss), and Mrs. Robinson. She was first married to Dr. Berkeley (Lord Berkeley's family) and secondly to Mr. Robinson, a man of good family and fortune. He died from a fall from his horse, hunting. She frequently visited at Ormesby. After her husband's death she adopted Annie Robinson, who afterwards became Mrs. Davidson. Sir William found everything gone, even the lead pipes which led water on to the house, which he restored at an expense of £400.

The old iron chest in the hall (a fac-simile I believe of one shewn at the Tower, and said to have been brought over at the date of the Spanish Armada) contained when left to Sir James £30,000 in sovereigns, which sum he spent in the course of a few months.

1864. Sept. 9. MEMORANDA BY JAMES WHITE PENNYMAN.

10. "Ormesby Hall,
9th Sept., 1864.

Memda. of the dates etc. of events which have happened of late years in our family made at the request of my son James Stovin Pennyman.

On the 17th Dec. 1761 my Grandfather James Worsley, Rector of Stonegrave, only brother of Thomas Worsley, of Hovingham Hall, married Dorothy Pennyman, youngest sister of Sir James Pennyman; Bt., of Ormesby Hall, and had issue James, born 14th April 1764, Ralph, bn. 7th July 1765, Richard, bn. 1st June 1767, Dorothy, bn. 6th Dec. 1775. My Grandfather had also the living of Gilling near Richmond; he died at Bath, and was buried in the Abbey Church at that place; my Grandmother was left in straightened circumstances (but was greatly assisted by her sister the wife of Wm. Bethell of Rise); she resided at York, where she died in 1811. My father James Worsley entered the army at an early age in the way common at that time vizt. as a Volunteer serving in the ranks (though associated with the Officers) untill a Commission should fall vacant, which soon occurred; he was with his Regiment, the 33rd, in Canada, and in what has since become the United States of America, where he served in the war of the rebellion; he was three years in America; he was then promoted to a Lieutenancy in the 2nd Queen's, which he joined at Gibraltar and remained there three years ; he went on half pay on being appointed to a company in the York Fencibles ; he was Lieut. Col. of that regiment at the time when it was disbanded in 1802. In 1783 he married Lydia, eldest daughter of Taylor White of Wallingwells; they went to reside at Wigthorpe, where I was born on the 15th Nov. 1792, but when he joined his regiment in Ireland she returned to Wallingwells, where her mother was then living with her son Sir Thos. Woollaston White. She with some of her children paid occasional visits to my father in Ireland; on his return to England in 1802, he took a house at Worksop; he shortly after was attacked with gout, from which he suffered dreadfully, and died of it in 1807. My Uncle Ralph was in orders; he had the livings of Ponton, Finchley, and St. Olaves, York, and was Subdean of Ripon ; the two latter were of no pecuniary benefit to him; he died at Ponton in 1848. My Uncle Richard entered the navy at an early age, and at his death held the rank of Vice Admiral; on being invalided from the West India Station when commanding the Intrepid—64 guns—he lived some years at North Stainley near Ripon; he afterwards bought some property near Tickhill, where he died in 1838. He married Elizabeth, my mother's sister. My Aunt Dorothy married the Rev. Nicholas Torre (who took 'the name of Holme), rectar of Rise ; she resided for some years at York in a state of widowhood, and died in 1858. After the marriage of my Uncle Sir Thos. White in 1801, my Grandmother White and her two unmarried daughters Sarah and Frances went to live at Wigthorpe ; in 1812 my Mother left Worksop, and went to live with her sisters at Wigthorpe. She died at Carlton in 1832. I and my brother Thomas were at an early age sent to school at Doncaster, where we remained till about 1803, and then as my father was residing at Worksop, we went as day scholars to a school at that place. I having been put on the list for a Woolwich Cadetship was removed to a school at Chelsea till 1807, when I joined at Marlow (where Tom already was as a Marlow Cadet). I joined at Woolwich in May 1808. Left Woolwich in Dec. 1811, and was on the survey in Berkshire till 1812 ; joined at Gosport 20 Aug. 1812, and at Chatham 19 May 1813, embarked at Portsmouth for Canada 25 Aug. 1813, landed at Quebec 6 Nov. 1813, was employed chiefly on the river Richelieu, Isle aux Noix, and Chambly, embarked at Quebec 11th Aug. 1815, landed at Deal 24th Sept., joined at Spike Island 23rd Oct. (with an interval of 5 months' leave of absence which I passed with my mother at Wigthorpe). I remained at Spike Island and Bere Island till 15 Oct. 1818, joined at Malta in June 1819, having gone there by way of France, Switzerland, Italy, and Sicily ; after remaining there a few months, I went to Corfu ; I several times shifted my quarters between Malta and the Ionian Islands, being employed chiefly on the survey of Corfu and Malta. On a reduction of part of the Corps of Royal Engineers, I was placed on half pay. I was promoted to the rank of Captain in 1826. I was appointed Sub-Inspector of Ionian Militia in 1827; that establishment was abolished in 1833, which again placed me on half pay. Sir Frederic Adam, the Lord High Commissioner of the Ionian Islands, had attached me to his Staff, and also procured for me the appointment of Intendent of Public Works in the Ionian Islands. In the autumn of 1827 I came home on leave, and on the 24th March 1828 was married at Cheltenham; on 2nd May left England with my wife for Corfu, where we arrived in June; we remained at Corfu till 1833, in the spring of which year my wife with our two children left me to go to England in consequence of the continued attacks of illness of Jem,* and in Sept. I followed. Dr. Stovin having died, we staid in England till Feby. 1834, when we returned to Corfu viâ Munich and Ancona. Shortly after my arrival, (Lord Nugent being then Lord High Commissioner,) I was informed that the place of Intendent of Public Works was to be discontinued. I however continued to stay at Corfu till the next spring, Jem still continuing very ill. In May 1835 we left Corfu and proceeded slowly to Baden Baden viâ Ancona, Pola, Trieste, Saybach, Meran, and Constanz; after a short stay at Baden we went to Heidelberg 4th Sept. 1835 and remained to the summer of 1836, when we returned to England viâ Rotterdam and Hull to my Brother Tom's at Hob Green; in the beginning of 1837 I was appointed Surveyor of Bridges of the North Riding; took a house at Thornton le Moor, where we continued to live till March 1853, when we removed to Ormesby.

(Signed)   JAS. W. PENNYMAN.

*James Stovin Pennyman.

Gc
929.2
P3847p
1836204

GENEALOGY
929.2
P3847P

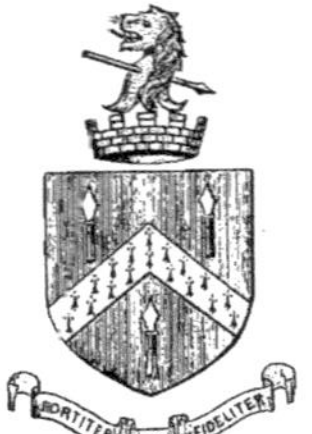

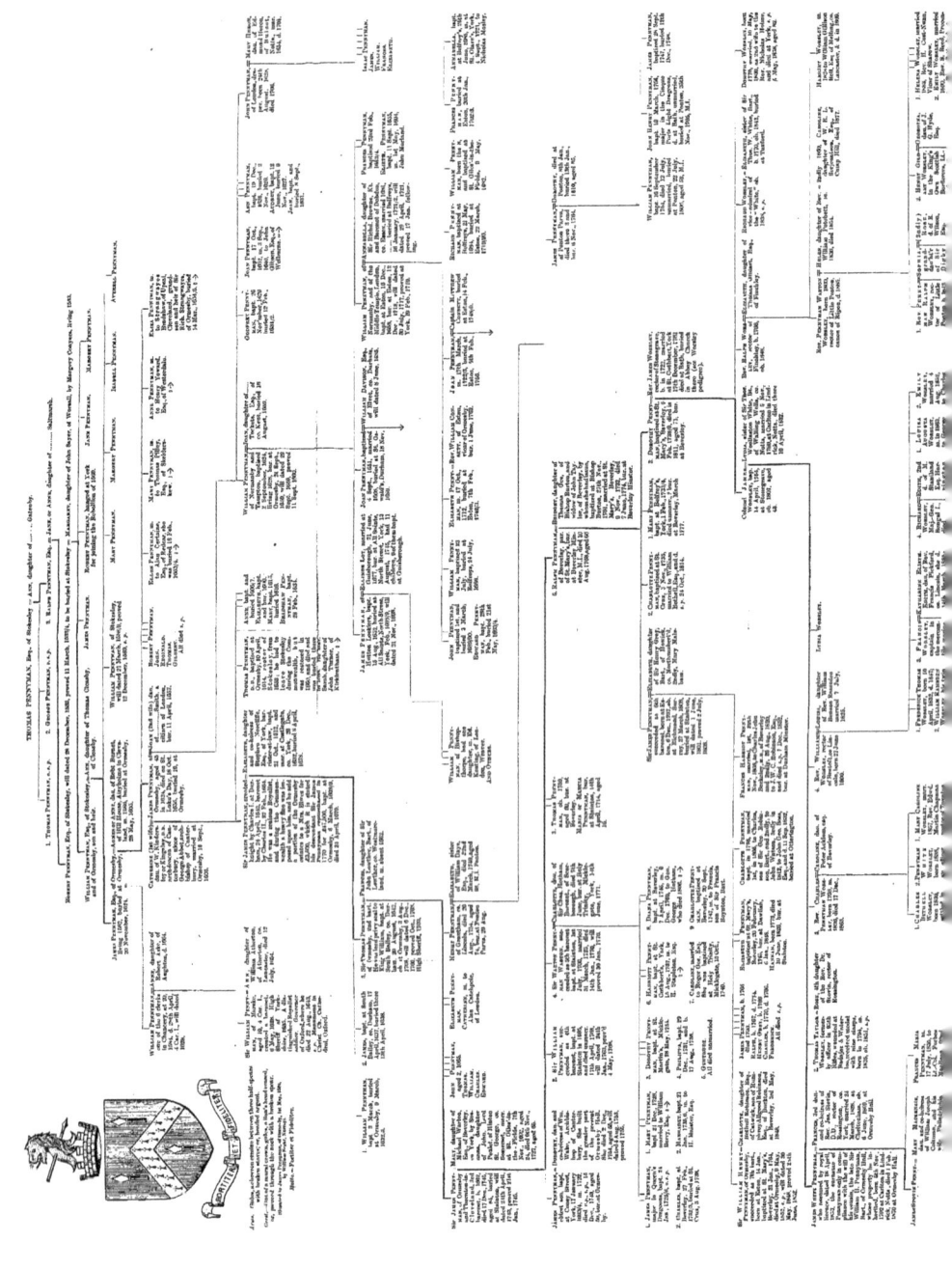

PENNYMAN OF ORMES

Pedigrees of Related Families.

NNYMAN OF ORMESBY.
Pedigrees of Related Families.

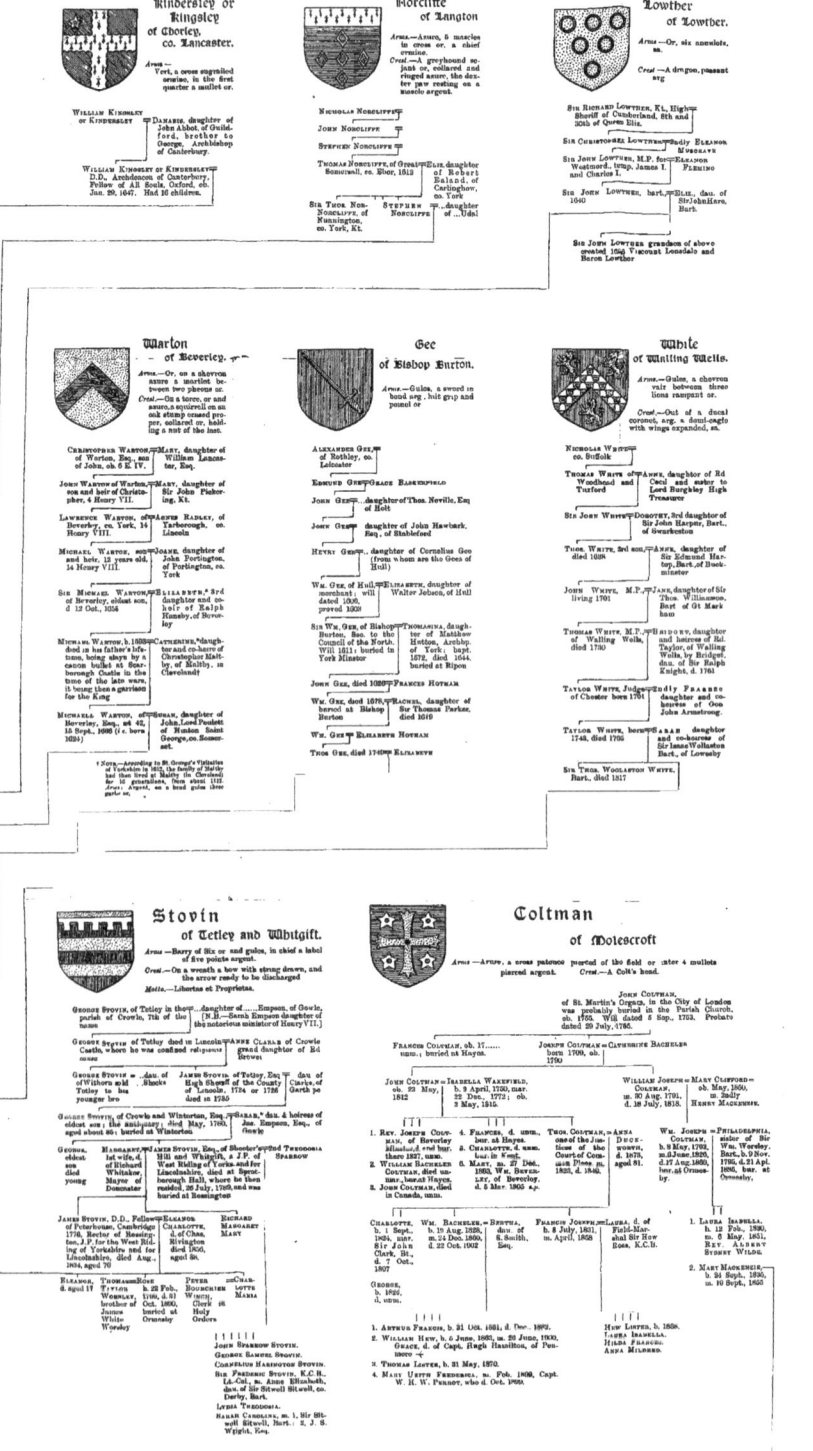

Kindersley or Kingsley of Chorley, co. Lancaster
Arms.—Vert, a cross engrailed ermine, in the first quarter a mullet or.

- WILLIAM KINGSLEY or KINDERSLEY = Damaris, daughter of John Abbot, of Guildford, brother to George, Archbishop of Canterbury.
- WILLIAM KINGSLEY of KINDERSLEY, D.D., Archdeacon of Canterbury, Fellow of All Souls, Oxford, ob. Jan. 29, 1647. Had 16 children.

Norcliffe of Langton
Arms.—Azure, 5 mascles in cross or, a chief ermine.
Crest.—A greyhound sejant or, collared and ringed azure, the dexter paw resting on a muscle argent.

- NICHOLAS NORCLIFFE
- JOHN NORCLIFFE
- STEPHEN NORCLIFFE
- THOMAS NORCLIFFE, of Great Somerwell, ob. Nber, 1613 = ELIZ. daughter of Robert Saland, of Carlinghow, co. York
- SIR THOS. NORCLIFFE, of Nunnington, co. York, Kt.
- STEPHEN NORCLIFFE = ...daughter of ...Udal

Lowther of Lowther
Arms.—Or, six annulets, sa.
Crest.—A dragon, passant arg.

- SIR RICHARD LOWTHER, Kt., High Sheriff of Cumberland, 8th and 30th of Queen Eliz.
- SIR CHRISTOPHER LOWTHER = ANNE, daughter of Lord Burghley High Treasurer MUSGRAVE
- SIR JOHN LOWTHER, M.P. for Westmorld., temp. James I. and Charles I. = ELEANOR FLEMING
- SIR JOHN LOWTHER, bart. 1640 = ELIZ., dau. of Sir John Hare, Bart.
- SIR JOHN LOWTHER grandson of above created 1694 Viscount Lonsdale and Baron Lowther

Warton of Beverley
Arms.—Or, on a chevron azure a martlet between two phoons arg.
Crest.—On a torce, or and azure, a squirrel on an oak stump erased proper, collared or, holding a nut of the last.

- CHRISTOPHER WARTON, of Warton, Esq., son of John, ob. 6 E. IV. = MARY, daughter of William Lancaster, Esq.
- JOHN WARTON of Warton, son and heir of Christopher, 4 Henry VII. = MARY, daughter of Sir John Pickering, Kt.
- LAWRENCE WARTON, of Beverley, co. York, 14 Henry VIII. = AGNES RADLEY, of Yarborough, co. Lincoln
- MICHAEL WARTON, son and heir, 15 years old, 14 Henry VIII. = JOANE, daughter of John Portington, of Portington, co. York
- SIR MICHAEL WARTON, of Beverley, eldest son, d. 12 Oct., 1655 = ELIZABETH, 3rd daughter and coheir of Ralph Rumsby, of Beverley
- MICHAEL WARTON, b. 1583 = CATHERINE, daughter and co-heir of Christopher Maltby, of Maltby, in Cleveland; died in his father's lifetime, being slayn by a canon bullet at Scarborough Castle in the time of the late wars, it being then a garrison for the King
- MICHAEL WARTON, of Beverley, Esq., æt 42, 15 Sept., 1665 (i.e. born 1624.) = SUSAN, daughter of John Lord Poulett of Hinton Saint Georges, co. Somerset.

Note.—According to St. George's Visitation of Yorkshire in 1612, the family of Warton had then lived at Maltby in Cleveland for 12 generations, from about 1112. Arms: Argent, on a bend gules three garbs or.

Gee of Bishop Burton
Arms.—Gules, a sword in bend arg., hilt grip and pomel or

- ALEXANDER GEE, of Rothley, co. Leicester
- EDMUND GEE = GRACE BASKERFIELD
- JOHN GEE = ...daughter of Thos. Neville, Esq. of Holt
- JOHN GEE = ...daughter of John Hawbark, Esq., of Stableford
- HENRY GEE = ...daughter of Cornelius Gee (from whom are the Gees of Hull)
- WM. GEE, of Hull = ELIZABETH, daughter of Walter Jobson, of Hull merchant; will dated 1606, proved 1608
- SIR WM. GEE, of Bishop Burton, Sec. to the Council of the North. Will 1611; buried in York Minster = THOMASINA, daughter of Matthew Hutton, Archbp. of York; bapt. 1572, died 1644, buried at Ripon
- JOHN GEE, died 1639 = FRANCES HOTHAM
- WM. GEE, died 1678 = RACHEL, daughter of Sir Thomas Parker, Bart.
- WM. GEE = ELIZABETH HOTHAM
- THOS. GEE, died 1740 = ELIZABETH

White of Walling Wells
Arms.—Gules, a chevron vair between three lions rampant or.
Crest.—Out of a ducal coronet, arg., a demi-eagle with wings expanded, sa.

- NICHOLAS WHITE, co. Suffolk
- THOMAS WHITE of Woodhead and Tuxford = ANNE, daughter of Rd Cecil and sister to Lord Burghley High Treasurer
- SIR JOHN WHITE = DOROTHY, 3rd daughter of Sir John Harper, Bart., of Swarkeston
- THOS. WHITE, 2nd son, died 1668 = ANNE, daughter of Sir Edmund Knatchbull, Bart., of Buckminster
- JOHN WHITE, M.P. = JANE, daughter of Sir Thos. Williamson, Bart. of Gt Markham living 1701
- THOMAS WHITE, M.P. of Walling Wells, died 1790 = BRIDGET, daughter and heiress of Rd. Taylor, of Walling Wells, by Bridget, dau. of Sir Ralph Knight, d. 1761
- TAYLOR WHITE, Judge of Chester born 1701 = EMILY FRASER daughter and coheiress of Geo John Armstrong.
- TAYLOR WHITE, born 1743, died 1795 = SARAH daughter and co-heiress of Sir Isaac Wollaston, Bart., of Loweeby
- SIR THOS. WOOLASTON WHITE, Bart., died 1817

Stovin of Tetley and Whitgift
Arms.—Barry of Six or and gules, in chief a label of five points argent.
Crest.—On a wreath a bow with strung drawn, and the arrow ready to be discharged.
Motto.—Libertas et Proprietas.

- GEORGE STOVIN, of Tetley in the parish of Crowle, 7th of Geo. 1 = ...daughter of ...Empson, of Gowle. (N.B.—Sarah Empson daughter of the notorious minister of Henry VII.)
- GEORGE STOVIN of Tetley died in Lincolnshire = ANNE CLARK of Crowle Castle, where he was confined religious grand daughter of Rd Steven
- GEORGE STOVIN of Crowle and Wintorton, Esq. = SARAH, dau. of ...Sheats Tetley to his younger bro
- JAMES STOVIN of Tetley, Esq. High Sheriff of the County of Lincoln, 1724 or 1726 died in 1740 = MARY dau of Clarke, of Garth parke
- GEORGE STOVIN, of Crowle and Winterton, Esq. = SARAH, dau. & heiress of eldest son; the antiquary; died May, 1780, aged about 85; buried at Winterton Jas. Empson, Esq., of Crowle
- GEORGIA, eldest, did unmarried
- HARRIET, of Richard Whitaker
- JAMES STOVIN, Esq. of West Riding of Yorks. and for Lincolnshire, died at Hall, where he resided, 26 July, 1789, and was buried at Rossington
- JOSEPH STOVIN = THEODOSIA SPARROW
- JAMES STOVIN, D.D., Fellow of Peterhouse, Cambridge, 1776, Rector of Blessington, J.P. for the West Riding of Yorkshire and for Lincolnshire, died Aug. 1834, aged 79 = ELEANOR daughter of Richard Bivington, died 1856, aged 68.
- ELEANOR = THOMAS HOWE WEMBLEY b. 28 Feb., 1798, d. 31 Jan., brother of Oct. 1880, James Wemsley
- PETER DRUM, buried at Holy Orensby
- CHARLOTTE MARIA, Clerk in Holy Orders
- JOHN SPARROW STOVIN
- GEORGE SAMUEL STOVIN
- CORNELIUS HARRINGTON STOVIN
- SIR FREDERICK STOVIN, K.C.B., Lt.-Col., m. Anne Elizabeth, dau. of Sir Sitwell Sitwell, Bart.
- LYDIA THEODOSIA
- SARAH CAROLINA, m. 1, Sir BROWELL SITWELL, Bart.; 2, J. S. Wright, Esq.

Coltman of Molescroft
Arms.—Azure, a cross patonce pearled of the field or inter 4 mullets pierced argent.

- JOHN COLTMAN of St. Martin's Organs, in the City of London was probably buried in the Parish Church, ob. 1753. Will dated 5 Sep., 1753. Probate dated 29 July, 1756.
- FRANCIS COLTMAN, ob. 17... unm., buried at Hayes
- JOSEPH COLTMAN = CATHERINE BACHELER born 1709, ob. 1790
- JOHN COLTMAN = ISABELLA WAKEFIELD ob. 30 May, m. 22 Dec., 1773; m. 1812 3 May, 1815.
- WILLIAM JOSEPH = MARY CLIFFORD COLTMAN, m. 30 Aug. 1791, m. 2ndly d. 19 July, 1818. HENRY MACKENZIE.
- 1. Rev. JOSEPH COLTMAN, of Beverley and Molescroft thereof 1837, unm.
- 2. WILLIAM BACHELER COLTMAN, died unm. at Hayes.
- 3. JOHN COLTMAN, died in Canada, unm.
- 4. FRANCES, d. unm., buried at Hayes.
- 5. CHARLOTTE, d. unm., bur. in Kent.
- 6. MARY, m. 27 Dec., 1853, Wm. BEVERLEY, of Beverley, d. 5 Mar. 1865 s.p.
- THOS. COLTMAN, ANNA one of the Justices of the Court of Common Pleas. ob. 1878, aged 81. = ELIZA, of Wm. WORSLEY Bart., b. 9 Nov. 1792, m. d. June 1826, d. 17 Aug. 1850, 1856, bur. at Ormesby.
- WM. JOSEPH = PHILADELPHIA, COLTMAN, sister of the b. 18 May, 1792, Wm. Worsley m. d.June 1826, Bart., b. 9 Nov. d. 17 Aug.1850, 1795, d. 21 Apl. 1856, bur. at Ormesby.
- 1. LAURA ISABELLA, b. 12 Feb., 1830, m. 5 May, 1851, REV. ALBERT SYDNEY WILDE.
- 2. MARY MACKENZIE, b. 24 Sept., 1836, m. 10 Sept., 1855
- CHARLOTTE, WM. BACHELER = BERTHA, FLAVEL, b. 24 Aug., 1828, m. 24 Dec. 1860, Sir John Clark, Bt., d. 7 Oct., 1867
- FRANCIS JOSEPH, CLAUDE, = LAURA d. of b. 8 July, 1831, Fieldhouse m. April, 1852 Marshal Sir Howe Ross, K.C.B.
- GEORGE, b. 1826, d. unm.
- 1. ARTHUR FRANCIS, b. 31 Oct. 1861, d. Dec., 1892.
- 2. WILLIAM HEW, b. 5 June, 1863, m. 26 June, 1900, GRACE, d. of Capt. Regd Hamilton, of Penshurst.
- 3. THOMAS LISTER, b. 31 May, 1870.
- 4. MARY EDITH FREDERICA, m. Feb. 1899, Capt. W. H. W. PEIRSE, who d. Oct. 1899.
- HEW LISTER, b. 1865.
- LAURA ISABELLA.
- HILDA FRANCES.
- ANNA MILDRED.

Beaumont (right column)

- WILLIAM DE BELLOMONT
- SIR RICHARD DE BELLOMONT
- SIR ROBERT DE BELLOMONT
- SIR JOHN DE BELLOMONT, Lord 21 Ed. III., settled lands in...
- HENRY DE BELLOMONT died early in...
- HENRY BEAUMONT, 5 Henry IV.
- RICHARD BEAUMONT, of Whitley Beaumont, d. 1742.
- THOMAS BEAUMONT, of Whitley Beaumont.
- RICHARD BEAUMONT, had a Crest granted to his ancient coat armour, 15 May, 1513.
- ROGER BEAUMONT = JOHANNA
- RICHARD BEAUMONT, d. 1673
- SIR RICHARD BEAUMONT, 1st knt. 1609, bart. 1628, d. 1631, unmarried.
- RICHARD BEAUMONT, of ANN LASCELLES Hall, d. 1656.
- SIR THOMAS BEAUMONT, KT., Governor of Sheffield Castle, 1643, d. 1668.
- RICHARD BEAUMONT, d. 1704.
- RICHARD BEAUMONT, Sheriff of Yorkshire 1713, d. 1723.
- RICHARD BEAUMONT, of ELLIOT Whitley Beaumont.
- JOHN BEAUMONT, b. 1782, d. 1836.
- CHARLES RICHARD BEAUMONT, d. of Whitley Beaumont d. 1813
- RICHARD HENRY = CATHERINE BEAUMONT, devised Whitley TIMOTHY WENTWORTH Beaumont to his godson HENRY FREDERICK BEAUMONT, the present possessor.
- WENTWORTH BLACKETT BEAUMONT